Mexican Favorites

GENERAL EDITOR
CHUCK WILLIAMS

RECIPES
SUSANNA PALAZUELOS

PHOTOGRAPHY
ALLAN ROSENBERG

TIME
LIFE
BOOKS

Time-Life Books is a division of
TIME LIFE INCORPORATED

President and CEO: John M. Fahey, Jr.
President, Time-Life Books: John D. Hall

TIME-LIFE CUSTOM PUBLISHING

Vice President and Publisher: Terry Newell
Sales Director: Frances C. Mangan
Editorial Director: Robert A. Doyle

WILLIAMS-SONOMA
Founder/Vice-Chairman: Chuck Williams

WELDON OWEN INC.
President: John Owen
Publisher: Wendely Harvey
Managing Editor: Laurie Wertz
Consulting Editor: Norman Kolpas
Copy Editor: Sharon Silva
Design/Editorial Assistant: Janique Poncelet
Design: John Bull, The Book Design Company
Production: Stephanie Sherman, James Obata,
    Mick Bagnato
Co-Editions Director: Derek Barton
Co-Editions Production Manager (US): Tarji Mickelson
Food Photographer: Allan Rosenberg
Additional Food Photography: Allen V. Lott
Primary Food & Prop Stylist: Sandra Griswold
Food Stylist: Heidi Gintner
Assistant Food Stylist: Danielle Di Salvo
Glossary Illustrations: Alice Harth

The Williams-Sonoma Kitchen Library
conceived and produced by Weldon Owen Inc.
814 Montgomery St., San Francisco, CA 94133

In collaboration with Williams-Sonoma
100 North Point, San Francisco, CA 94133

Production by Mandarin Offset, Hong Kong
Printed in China

A Note on Weights and Measures:
All recipes include customary U.S. and metric
measurements. Metric conversions are based on
a standard developed for these books and have
been rounded off. Actual weights may vary.

A Weldon Owen Production

Copyright © 1993 Weldon Owen Inc.
Reprinted in 1994; 1994; 1994; 1995

Library of Congress
Cataloging-in-Publication Data:

Palazuelos, Susanna.
    Mexican favorites / recipes, Susanna Palazuelos ;
photography, Allan Rosenberg.
        p.   cm. — (Williams-Sonoma kitchen library)
    Includes index.
    ISBN 0-7835-0270-2 ;
    ISBN 0-7835-0271-0 (lib. bdg.)
    1. Cookery, Mexican.   I. Title.   II. Series.
TX716.M4P34   1994
641.5972—dc20   93-28229
                                        CIP

Contents

Appetizers & Snacks 15

Light Lunch or Brunch 45

Casual Main Courses 83

INTRODUCTION

"No hay mejor salsa que un buen apetito," goes an old Mexican saying. "There's no better sauce than a hearty appetite."

In recent years, appetites worldwide in ever-growing numbers have turned to the foods of Mexico for flavorful satisfaction. Traditional Mexican cooking—with its lively spices, imaginative combinations of ingredients and casual yet festive presentation—perfectly meets a need when one seeks a change of pace in dining out.

And more and more people, when exposed to Mexican food in restaurants, are learning how easily that country's favorite recipes can be cooked at home. With that in mind, this book contains 45 authentic recipes for dishes beloved both within Mexico and beyond its borders. You'll find familiar tacos, enchiladas, burritos and tamales; recipes descended from Mayan and Aztec tradition, as well as some inspired by the nation's European heritage; and dishes that showcase the flair of contemporary Mexican cooks. Also included are instructions for making the tortillas, beans and salsas that bring extra character to the cuisine, and an illustrated glossary that will help you locate special ethnic ingredients—or find suitable substitutes.

As you glance through this book, I'm sure you'll be surprised at how familiar many of the recipes look. The reason lies partly in the fact that Mexican food has become a part of our lives. But more importantly, I think, it attests to the heartwarming honesty of simple food well prepared, regardless of its country of origin. Try these recipes once, and they're likely to become staples of your cooking repertoire.

Buen apetito.

EQUIPMENT

A host of familiar kitchen tools for turning out time-honored Mexican favorites

Most of the tools used to make traditional Mexican dishes are immediately familiar to modern-day cooks everywhere. Where Mexican specialties are concerned, however, some of these tools may be put to less familiar uses: a blender, for example, purées salsas; a potato masher produces creamy-soft refried beans; a rolling pin rolls out thin flour tortillas.

Just a few pieces of the equipment may require a trip to an ethnic market or a well-stocked kitchen equipment store: a tortilla press to streamline the preparation of the familiar flatbreads; and a molcajete sculpted from lava rock to yield the authentic consistency for traditional salsas.

1. Electric Blender
For rapid blending of sauces, select a sturdy model with an on-off switch and clear glass bowl that allow instantaneous control of a sauce's consistency.

2. Cast-iron Griddle
Sturdy griddle with shallow rim, for roasting chilies and other vegetables and for cooking tortillas. Use a flat, wooden or other nonmetal spatula for turning tortillas.

3. Grater/Shredder
For quick, easy grating or shredding of cheese to top a wide variety of dishes.

4. Meat Pounder
Small, sturdy metal disk with handle efficiently flattens pieces

of steak to wafer thinness for the traditional Mexican sandwiches known as *pepitos*.

5. Potato Masher
For mashing of refried beans or guacamole. Choose a sturdy masher made of stainless steel.

6. Electric Spice Mill
For freshly ground spices or seeds, use a good-quality electric spice mill or coffee mill with a fingertip control.

7. Small Saucepan
For cooking sauces and small quantities of other ingredients.

8. Chef's Knife and Paring Knife

An 8- or 10-inch (20- or 25-cm) chef's knife chops and slices large items or large quantities of ingredients; a 3½–4-inch (9–10-cm) paring knife peels vegetables and cuts up small ingredients.

9. Tortilla Press

Hinged, heavy-duty aluminum device quickly and neatly presses out uniform, circular corn tortillas from homemade dough.

10. Electric Tortilla Maker

Self-heating appliance flattens and then cooks tortillas in one easy step.

11. Baking Dishes

For oven-baked recipes, select heavy-duty glazed porcelain, stoneware, earthenware or glass in a range of sizes.

12. Metal Tongs

For easy, efficient and safe turning of foods as they fry in hot oil, choose long-handled, spring-hinged heavy-duty tongs.

13. Slotted Spoon

For turning, lifting and draining foods fried in hot oil.

14. Heavy Frying Pan

For frying tortillas, pan-roasting chilies and other vegetables, toasting pumpkin seeds, shallow frying and general-purpose sautéing of ingredients.

15. Large Saucepan

For simmering beans, steaming tamales and cooking poultry or meat for tortilla fillings.

16. Mixing Bowls

Sturdy bowls in a range of sizes for mixing ingredients and for serving dips and salsas. Can be made of glass, porcelain, earthenware or stainless steel.

17. Steamer Basket

Petaled, flowerlike shape enables the basket to expand or contract to fit saucepans of various sizes, for holding cornhusk-wrapped tamales as they steam above simmering water. Small center post is used to lift the basket out of the pan after cooking.

18. Molcajete

Traditional Mexican lava-rock mortar and pestle for hand-grinding salsas to a coarse, rustic consistency.

19. Food Processor

For general preparation of ingredients in large quantities, and for rapid blending of sauces.

20. Wooden Spoons

All-purpose tools for stirring. Choose good-quality spoons with sturdy handles.

21. Basting Brush

For basting foods as they marinate, grill or broil. Choose a sturdy brush with well-attached natural bristles.

22. Dowel-Type Rolling Pin

For rolling out flour tortillas on a work surface, select a sturdy hardwood pin. To prevent warping, do not wash; wipe clean with a dry cloth.

Corn Tortillas

Tortillas de Maiz

Nothing beats the flavor and texture of hot, freshly made corn tortillas, an accompaniment to almost every Mexican meal. In Mexico, most people buy them from nearby shops or factories that always have a fresh supply. If you can't find freshly made tortillas, this simple recipe will produce authentic results. A tortilla press, available in Mexican markets and in well-stocked cookware stores, makes the job go quickly and easily; alternatively, use a rolling pin to roll out the tortillas between two sheets of waxed paper. To store cooked tortillas, let cool, enclose in plastic wrap and refrigerate for 2–3 days or freeze for several weeks. To reheat, place on a griddle or nonstick frying pan over medium-high heat, or enclose in plastic wrap and place in a microwave oven for about 30 seconds.

2 cups (10 oz/315 g) masa harina
about 1½ cups (12 fl oz/375 ml) lukewarm water

1. Mixing the dough.
In a mixing bowl, use your fingertips to work together masa harina and lukewarm water to form a soft, non-sticky dough. Form the dough into a ball.

2. Kneading the dough.
Cover the dough with a kitchen towel and let it rest for 5–10 minutes. Then, on a work surface, knead it with the heel of your hand for 2–3 minutes.

Place the masa harina in a large bowl. Add the lukewarm water all at once, working it into the flour to form a dough that is soft but does not stick to your fingers. Form the dough into a ball and cover the bowl with a kitchen towel. Let stand for 5–10 minutes.

On a work surface, knead the dough for 2–3 minutes. Divide the dough into 12 portions. Rolling each portion between the palms of your hands, form it into a ball about 1½ inches (4 cm) in diameter. Cover the lower surface of an opened tortilla press with a piece of plastic wrap that extends beyond its edges and place a ball of dough in the center. Cover the ball with another piece of plastic wrap of equal size. Lower the top of the press and push down gently. The tortilla should be about 5 inches (13 cm) in diameter and 1/16 inch (2 mm) thick.

Open the tortilla press and peel off the top sheet of plastic wrap. Using the bottom sheet, lift the tortilla from the press and turn it over onto your hand. Peel off the bottom sheet of plastic wrap. Heat a dry, heavy frying pan or griddle over medium-high heat. Gently place the tortilla onto the preheated frying pan or griddle. As soon as the edges start to dry out, after about 20 seconds, turn over the tortilla. Cook on the second side until lightly browned, 15–20 seconds. Turn the tortilla again and cook a few seconds more. Transfer to one end of a kitchen towel. As the tortillas are cooked, stack them and cover completely with the other half of the towel to keep them warm and moist until serving.

Makes about 1 lb (500 g) dough, or 12 tortillas

3. Forming individual portions.
By hand, divide and roll the dough into 1½-inch (4-cm) balls. Put one on the lower plate of a tortilla press lined with plastic wrap.

4. Pressing tortillas.
Cover the ball with another sheet of plastic wrap and close the press to flatten the tortilla. Open the press and peel away the plastic wrap.

5. Cooking the tortillas.
On a preheated griddle or frying pan, cook the tortilla until it starts to brown and its edges begin to dry, about 20 seconds per side. Continue pressing and cooking the remaining tortillas in the same manner.

Totopos
TORTILLA CHIPS

These crisply fried triangles of corn tortilla are more typically known outside of Mexico as tostaditas or tortilla or taco chips. A favorite companion of many recipes in this collection, they are also delicious dipped into salsas (recipes on pages 12–13), guacamole (page 25) or a spicy cheese dip (page 20). Once fried, totopos can be allowed to cool and then stored in an airtight container for up to 2 days.

corn oil or other vegetable oil for frying
corn tortillas, each cut into 6 wedges

*I*n a frying pan over high heat, pour in oil to a depth of about 1½ inches (4 cm). Heat until the oil is smoking. Working in batches, add the tortilla wedges and fry until crisp and golden, about 1 minute.

Using a slotted spoon, transfer to paper towels to drain.

Crab Meat Tacos

Flour Tortillas

TORTILLAS DE HARINA

Flour tortillas are a specialty of northern Mexico, the principal wheat-growing region of the country. Make a stack of them and keep on hand for spur-of-the-moment meals. To store cooked tortillas, let cool, seal in plastic wrap and refrigerate for 2–3 days or freeze for several weeks. Reheat in a nonstick frying pan or on a griddle over medium-high heat. Or enclose in plastic wrap and place in a microwave oven for about 30 seconds.

2–2¼ cups (8–9 oz/250–280 g) all-purpose (plain)
   flour, sifted before measuring
¼ cup (2 oz/60 g) vegetable shortening or lard
1 teaspoon salt
1 cup (8 fl oz/250 ml) warm water

*I*n a mixing bowl combine 2 cups (8 oz/250 g) flour, the shortening or lard and salt. Using your fingers, rub the ingredients together until the mixture has the consistency of fine crumbs. Gradually add the warm water, stirring it in with a fork, and continue to mix until the ingredients come together to form a soft dough. Add the remaining ¼ cup (1 oz/30 g) flour if the mixture is sticking to your fingers.

Alternatively, combine the flour, shortening or lard and salt in a food processor fitted with the metal blade. Process to form fine crumbs. Add the warm water, ¼ cup (2 fl oz/60 ml) at a time, and process until the ingredients form a soft mass around the blade.

Gather up the dough, pat it into a ball and place in a bowl. Knead the dough inside the bowl until elastic, about 2 minutes. Cover with a kitchen towel and let stand at room temperature for 2 hours.

Break off small pieces of the dough and, rolling each piece between your palms, form into balls 1½ inches (4 cm) in diameter. On a floured board, using a rolling pin, roll out each ball into a thin round 6–7 inches

(15–18 cm) in diameter. As you roll out the tortillas, turn them over a few times and add flour to the surface as needed to prevent sticking.

Heat a dry, heavy frying pan or griddle over medium heat. Place a tortilla on the pan or griddle and cook until it looks dry and the underside begins to brown, about 30 seconds. Turn the tortilla over and cook the second side until browned, about 30 seconds. Transfer the tortilla to one end of a kitchen towel. As the tortillas are cooked, stack them and cover completely with the other half of the towel to keep them warm and moist until serving.

Makes about 24 tortillas

Rolling out a flour tortilla
Made from a dough more elastic than that used for corn tortillas, flour tortillas are rolled out rather than pressed. Place the balls of dough on a floured work surface and roll out using the firm, steady pressure of a rolling pin.

Pot Beans

FRIJOLES DE OLLA

Beans, one of the staples of the Mexican kitchen, are traditionally simmered in a clay pot, although modern cooks often use a pressure cooker to cut the cooking time. An epazote sprig is a classic addition to the pot, but easier-to-locate cilantro is a good substitute. The cooked beans will keep in an airtight container in the refrigerator for 2–3 days.

2 cups (14 oz/440 g) dried black, pinto or pink beans
2½ qt (2.5 l) water
⅓ onion
3 tablespoons lard or bacon drippings
1 fresh cilantro (fresh coriander) or epazote sprig
2 teaspoons salt, plus salt to taste
3 fresh serrano chili peppers

*R*inse the beans under cold running water and place in a bowl. Add water to cover by 2 inches (5 cm) and let soak for about 3 hours.

Discard any beans that are floating, then drain the beans and place in a large, heavy pot. Add the 2½ qt (2.5 l) water, onion and lard or drippings and bring to a boil. Cover, reduce the heat to medium and boil until the beans are tender, 1½–2 hours. Make sure the beans are always well covered with water, adding more hot water as needed.

When the beans are tender, add the cilantro or epazote, the 2 teaspoons salt and the chilies. Simmer uncovered for 20 minutes longer. Discard the onion, herb sprig and chilies. Adjust the seasoning, then serve.

Makes about 5 cups (40 fl oz/1.25 l); serves 6

Refried Beans

FRIJOLES REFRITOS

Mashed and then fried until all their liquid is gone, pot beans become refried beans. Traditionally the beans are fried in lard, but vegetable oil is used here to eliminate the cholesterol. Serve with totopos *(recipe on page 9).*

½ cup (4 fl oz/125 ml) vegetable oil
½ onion, cut into chunks
pot beans with their liquid *(recipe at left)*
crumbled *queso fresco* or feta cheese, optional

*I*n a large frying pan over medium heat, warm the oil. Add the onion and sauté until soft, about 2 minutes. Discard the onion. Add half of the beans with their liquid and, using a potato masher, mash them until they form a coarse purée. Gradually add the remaining beans and liquid and continue mashing until all the beans are coarsely puréed.

Raise the heat to medium-high and cook, stirring, until the purée begins to dry out, 3–5 minutes.

Transfer to a warmed platter and sprinkle with the crumbled cheese, if desired. Serve immediately.

Makes about 5 cups (40 fl oz/1.25 l); serves 6

Pot Beans

Refried Beans

Fresh Mexican Salsa

SALSA MEXICANA

The key to making this classic table condiment lies in chopping all the fresh ingredients by hand.

3 ripe tomatoes, finely chopped
½ cup (2 oz/60 g) chopped onion
4–6 fresh serrano chili peppers, seeded and finely chopped
1 tablespoon finely chopped fresh cilantro (fresh coriander)
2 teaspoons salt
2 teaspoons fresh lime juice

*I*n a bowl stir together the tomatoes, onion, chilies, cilantro, salt and lime juice. Let stand for 1 hour, to blend the flavors before serving. The salsa can be stored tightly covered in the refrigerator for up to 1 week.

Makes about 1½ cups (12 fl oz/375 ml)

Fresh Mexican Salsa

Red Picante Salsa

SALSA PICANTE ROJA

Typical of Tex-Mex cuisine, this cooked salsa shows Mexico's influence on the kitchens of the American Southwest. It makes a fine condiment for many recipes in this book and is also excellent with grilled meat, chicken or seafood. If you'd like a hotter salsa, feel free to increase the quantity of pickled chilies.

4 small ripe tomatoes, peeled and coarsely chopped
½ cup (2 oz/60 g) coarsely chopped onion
2 cloves garlic
1 canned pickled jalapeño chili pepper, plus 1 tablespoon liquid from can
1 tablespoon corn oil or other vegetable oil
½ teaspoon dried oregano, crumbled
½ teaspoon salt

*I*n a blender or in a food processor fitted with the metal blade, combine the tomatoes, onion, garlic and chili. Purée until smooth.

In a saucepan over medium heat, warm the oil. Add the tomato mixture, chili liquid, oregano and salt. Cook uncovered, stirring occasionally, until the mixture thickens slightly, about 10 minutes. Remove from the heat and let cool completely.

Transfer to a bowl and serve. The salsa can be stored tightly covered in the refrigerator for up to 1 week.

Makes about 1½ cups (12 fl oz/375 ml)

Red Picante Salsa

Tomatillo Salsa
SALSA DE TOMATE VERDE

Found on most tables in Mexican homes and restaurants, this versatile condiment enhances any savory dish. It is made with tomatillos, which are known in Mexico as tomates verdes; *and although they aren't, in fact, related to tomatoes, their size, shape and texture are similar. You'll find them fresh, covered in their brown papery husks, in ethnic markets, well-stocked food stores, or in fruit and vegetable shops; they are also sold canned.*

3 cups (24 fl oz/750 ml) water
2½ teaspoons salt
2 cloves garlic
4 fresh serrano chili peppers
1 lb (500 g) tomatillos, husks removed
½ cup (¾ oz/20 g) loosely packed fresh cilantro (fresh
   coriander) sprigs
¼ cup (1¼ oz/37 g) finely chopped onion

In a saucepan over high heat, combine the water and 1 teaspoon of the salt and bring to a boil. Add the garlic, chilies and tomatillos and cook, uncovered, until soft, 8–10 minutes. Drain, reserving ½ cup (4 fl oz/ 125 ml) of the liquid. When cool enough to handle, stem the chilies and tomatillos.

  In a blender or in a food processor fitted with the metal blade, combine the garlic, chilies, tomatillos, reserved liquid, cilantro and the remaining 1½ tea- spoons salt. Process to form a smooth purée, then transfer to a bowl. Stir in the chopped onion.

  Let the salsa cool to room temperature, then serve. The salsa can be stored tightly covered in the refrigerator for up to 1 week.

Makes 2 cups (16 fl oz/500 ml)

Red Molcajete Salsa
SALSA DE MOLCAJETE ROJA

A popular condiment throughout Mexico, except in the Yucatán, this salsa has a rich flavor enhanced by roasting the chilies and tomatoes. It goes well with many of the recipes in this collection. If you can, use a molcajete—a mortar made from lava rock—to give the salsa a more traditional, rustic texture and flavor.

5 fresh serrano chili peppers
2 ripe tomatoes
1 clove garlic
1 teaspoon salt

Heat a dry, heavy frying pan or griddle over medium heat. Place the chilies and tomatoes on the pan or griddle and roast, turning occasionally, until they are well charred and slightly softened, 5–8 minutes, depending upon their size. Remove from the heat and, when cool enough to handle, stem the chilies and tomatoes.

  In a blender or in a food processor fitted with the metal blade, combine the roasted tomatoes and chilies, garlic and salt. Process until chopped into small chunks; do not purée. Transfer to a bowl and serve. The salsa can be stored tightly covered in the refrigerator for up to 1 week.

*Makes about 1½ cups
(12 fl oz/375 ml)*

Red Molcajete Salsa

Tomatillo Salsa

13

Deep-Fried Chilies Stuffed with Cream Cheese

CHILES PORTANOVA

2 cups (16 fl oz/500 ml) corn oil or other vegetable oil

12 fresh jalapeño or yellow wax chili peppers

1 cup (8 fl oz/250 ml) water

½ cup (4 fl oz/125 ml) distilled white vinegar

½ teaspoon salt

3 oz (90 g) cream cheese

⅓ cup (2 oz/60 g) all-purpose (plain) flour

1 egg, lightly beaten

½ cup (2 oz/50 g) freshly grated Parmesan cheese

red picante salsa or red molcajete salsa (recipes on pages 12–13)

The Baronessa di Portanova loves to make this hors d'oeuvre when she entertains at her estate in Acapulco. Although jalapeño or wax chilies are normally quite fiery, deribbing, seeding and then soaking them for 24 hours tempers their hotness without diminishing their flavor.

The day before serving, place the oil in a small frying pan over high heat and heat until very hot. Add the chilies, a few at a time, and fry until well blistered, about 3 seconds on each side. Using a slotted spoon transfer the chilies to a large bowl filled with cold water. Remove the pan from the heat and let the oil cool, then reserve in a covered container for cooking the stuffed chilies the next day. With the chilies still in the water, peel off the skins with your fingers, or use a knife if necessary. Then make a lengthwise slit in each one and remove the seeds and ribs; leave stem intact. Discard the water.

In a bowl stir together the 1 cup (8 fl oz/250 ml) water, vinegar and salt. Add the chilies, cover and let soak at room temperature for 24 hours to reduce the piquancy.

Drain the chilies, rinse under cold water and drain again; pat dry. Carefully stuff each chili with an equal amount of the cream cheese. Place the flour, egg and Parmesan cheese in separate shallow bowls. Dip the stuffed chilies, one at a time, first in the flour, then in the beaten egg and finally in the cheese, coating completely each time.

Pour the reserved oil into a small frying pan over medium heat. When the oil is hot, add the chilies, a few at a time, and fry until lightly golden, about 2 minutes on each side. Using a slotted spoon, transfer to paper towels to drain. Serve warm with salsa on the side.

Makes 12 stuffed chilies

Jicama, Cucumber and Mango with Orange and Chili

Pico de Gallo

2 large jicamas, about 1½ lb (750 g) total weight

2 large cucumbers

1 large firm ripe mango

2 large seedless oranges

⅓ cup (3 fl oz/80 ml) fresh lime juice

1 teaspoon chili powder, or to taste

1 teaspoon salt

1 fresh serrano chili pepper, finely chopped (optional)

3 limes, cut into wedges

6 fresh mint sprigs

The Spanish name means "rooster's beak," an evocative reference to the sharp flavors of lime juice and chili powder that season this refreshing, tangy appetizer. Normally only oranges and jicama are used, but this more elaborate version includes cucumber and mango slices; if pineapple is in season, it may also be included. Offer tequila or margaritas or other refreshing cocktails.

Peel and slice the jicamas ½ inch (12 mm) thick, then cut into sticks 3 inches (7.5 cm) long and ½ inch (12 mm) wide. Cut the cucumbers in half crosswise. Peel them, then cut in half lengthwise. Scoop out the seeds and discard. Cut the cucumbers into sticks the same size as the jicama sticks. Peel and pit the mango (see glossary), then slice lengthwise. Peel the oranges and remove the white membranes. Slice the oranges crosswise.

Attractively arrange the jicama and cucumber sticks and the mango and orange slices on a large platter. Pour the lime juice evenly over the top and then sprinkle with the chili powder, salt and chopped chili (if using). Garnish with lime wedges and mint sprigs.

Serves 6

Cornmeal Boats with Pork or Chicken Filling

CHALUPAS

3 cups (15 oz/470 g) masa harina

½ teaspoon salt

⅓ cup (3 fl oz/80 ml) plus 2 tablespoons corn oil or other vegetable oil or melted vegetable shortening

1½ cups (12 fl oz/375 ml) lukewarm water

1 cup (5 oz/155 g) shredded, cooked pork or chicken

½ cup (2½ oz/75 g) finely chopped onion

1 cup (5 oz/155 g) crumbled *queso fresco* or feta cheese

fresh Mexican salsa or tomatillo salsa (recipes on pages 12–13)

A dish from the state of Puebla, chalupas, *which are thicker and crisper than tortillas, take their name and shape from a small, two-person canoe.*

*P*lace the masa harina in a bowl. Add the salt, the ⅓ cup (3 fl oz/ 80 ml) oil or shortening and the water. Using your fingers, mix to form a soft dough that is not sticky. Divide into 12 equal balls. Roll each ball into a strip 5½ inches (14 cm) by ½ inch (12 mm).

Cover the lower surface of an opened tortilla press with a sheet of plastic wrap that extends beyond its edges and place a dough strip in the center. Cover with a sheet of plastic wrap. Lower the top and push down gently. The *chalupa* should be an oval ⅛ inch (3 mm) thick.

Open the tortilla press and peel off the top sheet of plastic wrap. Using the bottom sheet, lift the *chalupa* from the press and turn it over onto your hand. Peel off the bottom sheet. Meanwhile, heat a heavy frying pan or griddle over medium-high heat. Gently place the *chalupa* on the preheated surface. Cook until the edges begin to dry out, about 45 seconds. Turn and cook the second side until lightly browned, about 45 seconds, at the same time pinching up the edges of the cooked side to form a rim. Turn once again and cook the first side until the edges begin to brown, 45–60 seconds. Transfer to a plate and cover with a cloth until all the *chalupas* are ready. (At this point you can set them aside for up to 3 hours.)

Just before serving, preheat the pan or griddle over medium-high heat. Place the *chalupas*, a few at a time and rim sides up, on the hot surface and drizzle evenly with the 2 tablespoons oil or shortening. They are warmed through when the oil begins to sizzle. Transfer to individual plates and top with the meat, onion, cheese and salsa.

Serves 6

Tex-Mex Cheese Dip with Tortilla Chips

DIP TEX-MEX CON TOTOPOS

1 cup (4 oz/125 g) shredded Cheddar
cheese
1 cup (4 oz/125 g) finely diced processed
American cheese
2 tablespoons finely chopped canned
pickled jalapeño chili pepper
2 tablespoons finely chopped red bell
pepper (capsicum)
totopos made from 6 corn tortillas
(recipe on page 9)

*Quickly and easily prepared, this American-style dip of melted
cheese shows a strong Mexican influence. It can also be used for
dipping vegetable sticks such as celery, carrot or bell pepper. Serve
with beer or margaritas.*

Combine the cheeses in the top pan of a double boiler or in
a heatproof bowl. Place over simmering water until melted,
about 5 minutes. Alternatively, combine the cheeses in a
microwave-safe container and place in a microwave oven set
on high for 2–3 minutes.

Add the chili and bell pepper to the melted cheeses and stir
to mix well.

To serve, place the *totopos* on a platter. Transfer the hot
cheese dip to a bowl and nest it on the platter with the *totopos*.
Serve immediately.

Serves 6

Crisp Tortilla Packets with Pork
CHILINDRINAS

1 head garlic, loose outer peel removed

1 onion, cut in half

5 cups (40 fl oz/1.25 l) water

1 teaspoon dried oregano, crumbled

½ teaspoon salt, plus 2 tablespoons salt

1 lb (500 g) pork tenderloin, cut into
2-inch (5-cm) chunks

2 lb (1 kg) ripe tomatoes, coarsely
chopped

1 tablespoon corn oil or other vegetable
oil, plus oil for frying

5 tablespoons (2½ oz/70 g) well-drained
capers, minced

⅓ cup (2 oz/60 g) minced green olives

2 lb (1 kg) dough for corn tortillas
(recipe on page 8)

shredded lettuce

½ cup (2 oz/60 g) shredded Cheddar
cheese

The colloquial Mexican name for this popular Yucatán appetizer means "trifle" or "a bit of fun."

Heat a dry, heavy frying pan or griddle over medium heat. Roast the garlic head and half of the onion, turning occasionally, until evenly charred, 4–5 minutes.

Transfer the charred garlic and onion to a saucepan and add the water, oregano, the ½ teaspoon salt and the pork. Bring to a boil, reduce the heat to medium-low, cover and simmer until the pork is tender, 45–50 minutes. Remove the pork and let cool completely. Using your fingers or two forks, shred the meat; set aside.

In a blender or in a food processor fitted with the metal blade, combine the tomatoes, the remaining onion half and the 2 table-spoons salt. Purée until smooth. In a saucepan over medium heat, warm the 1 tablespoon oil; add the purée. Cook uncovered, stirring often, to form a medium-thick consistency, about 10 minutes.

In a bowl stir together 2 cups (16 fl oz/500 ml) of the sauce, the capers, olives and pork; set aside. Keep the remaining sauce warm.

Following the directions for forming tortillas on pages 8–9, divide the dough into 24 balls each about 1½ inches (4 cm) in diameter and then press into tortillas about 5 inches (13 cm) in diameter. Spoon 2 tablespoons pork mixture onto the center of each tortilla, fold in the sides, then fold over the ends and press closed.

In a small frying pan over high heat, pour in oil to a depth of ½ inch (12 mm). When hot, fry the filled tortillas, a few at a time and turning once, until golden, about 2 minutes on each side. Transfer to paper towels to drain briefly. Line plates with lettuce and top with the tortilla packets. Spoon on the warm sauce, sprinkle with the cheese and serve.

Serves 6

Guacamole

2 large ripe avocados
1 tablespoon finely chopped onion
1 or 2 fresh serrano chili peppers, finely
  chopped
1 large ripe tomato, peeled and finely
  chopped
2 fresh cilantro (fresh coriander) sprigs,
  finely chopped
fresh lime juice
salt

Although you can mash it in a bowl with a fork or potato masher, this classic dip or garnish of ripe avocados, onion, chilies, tomatoes and cilantro tastes wonderful when made in and served from a molcajete—Mexico's traditional lava-rock mortar. To reduce the hotness of the dish, seed the chili peppers before chopping them. Accompany the guacamole with totopos (recipe on page 9) or raw vegetables for dipping.

Cut each avocado in half, remove the pits and scoop out the pulp into a bowl. Mash lightly with a fork.

Add the onion, chilies, tomato and cilantro and stir with a fork until well mixed. Season to taste with lime juice and salt.

Serve immediately, as guacamole gradually darkens when exposed to the air.

Makes about 2 cups (1 lb/500 g); serves 6

Fried Tortilla Puffs with Chicken
SALBUTES

½ lb (250 g) red (Spanish) onion, finely
   minced (about 1⅔ cups)
1 cup (8 fl oz/250 ml) apple cider vinegar
1 whole chicken breast or 2 breast halves
1 cup (5 oz/155 g) masa harina
1 cup (5 oz/155 g) all-purpose (plain)
   flour
1⅓ cups (11 fl oz/330 ml) lukewarm
   water
vegetable oil for frying
1 ripe tomato, thinly sliced
1 ripe avocado, halved, pitted, peeled and
   sliced lengthwise

*Frying puffs up the thick flour-and-cornmeal tortillas that form the base
for this popular appetizer from Mérida, a city in the Yucatán. Make the
typical red-onion relish the day before, so its flavors can develop fully.
Substitute leftover turkey, pork or beef for the chicken, if you wish.*

*T*he day before serving, combine the red onion with the vinegar in
a glass bowl. Cover and refrigerate.

Place the chicken in a saucepan and add water to cover. Bring
to a boil, reduce the heat to medium-low, cover and cook until
tender, about 25 minutes. Drain and let cool completely. Bone and
skin the chicken, then, using your fingers or two forks, shred the
meat. Set aside.

Place the masa harina and flour in a large bowl. Add the water,
using your fingers to work it into the flours to form a dough. The
dough should be soft but not stick to your fingers. Form into 12
balls each about 2 inches (5 cm) in diameter.

Following the directions for forming tortillas on pages 8–9, press
the balls into tortillas about 4 inches (10 cm) in diameter and
⅛ inch (3 mm) thick.

In a frying pan over high heat, pour in oil to a depth of ½ inch
(12 mm). When the oil is hot, fry the tortillas, one at a time, until a
very light gold, about 25 seconds on each side. Transfer to paper
towels to drain. Keep warm.

To serve, place 2 tortillas on each plate. Top with the shredded
chicken. Using a slotted spoon to drain off some of the vinegar, top
with the minced red onion relish. Garnish with the tomato and
avocado slices.

Serves 6

Marinated Jalapeño Chilies

CHILES JALAPEÑOS EN ESCABECHE

1 tablespoon vegetable oil

2 lb (1 kg) fresh jalapeño chili peppers

1 large onion, thinly sliced

1 head garlic, cut in half vertically and loose outer peel removed

2 large carrots, peeled and thinly sliced

3 cups (24 fl oz/750 ml) distilled white vinegar

1 cup (8 fl oz/250 ml) water

3 rounded tablespoons dried oregano, crumbled

¼ cup (2 oz/60 g) firmly packed dark brown sugar

salt and freshly ground pepper

Homemade pickled chilies are easy to make and keep well for months in the refrigerator, ready to serve on an hors d'oeuvre tray, to accompany grilled steaks or chicken, or to cut into strips for tucking into tacos. A jar of chilies also makes a charming gift for food-loving friends.

*I*n a large saucepan over medium heat, warm the oil. Add the chilies, onion, garlic and carrot and sauté until tender-crisp, about 1 minute. Add the vinegar, water, oregano, brown sugar and salt and pepper to taste and bring to a boil. Remove from the heat, cover and let cool completely before serving.

To store, pour into glass jars and cover tightly. The pickled chilies can be refrigerated for up to 3 months.

Makes about 8 cups (64 fl oz/2 l)

Mushroom Quesadillas

QUESADILLAS DE HONGOS

FOR THE MUSHROOM FILLING:

2 tablespoons unsalted butter

¼ cup (2 fl oz/60 ml) olive oil

3 cloves garlic, finely chopped

½ onion, finely chopped

2 fresh serrano chili peppers, finely
chopped

1 lb (500 g) fresh mushrooms, sliced

2 tablespoons finely chopped fresh
cilantro (fresh coriander) or 1 tablespoon finely chopped fresh epazote

salt and freshly ground pepper

1 lb (500 g) dough for corn tortillas
  (recipe on page 8)

3 tablespoons all-purpose (plain) flour

1 tablespoon vegetable shortening or lard,
melted

1 teaspoon baking powder

½ teaspoon salt

corn oil or other vegetable oil for frying

*Come summer in central Mexico, the popular cheese-filled corn tortillas
are instead stuffed with wild mushrooms. This recipe calls for cultivated
mushrooms, but you can substitute your favorite wild variety. If you
prefer to make cheese quesadillas, fill each tortilla with 1½ tablespoons
cheese of your choice and a sprig of epazote or cilantro. Serve with your
choice of salsas (recipes on pages 12–13) or guacamole (page 25).*

To make the mushroom filling, in a frying pan over medium heat,
melt the butter with the oil. Add the garlic and onion and sauté
until golden, about 2 minutes. Add the chilies, mushrooms and
cilantro or epazote and sauté until the mushrooms are tender,
about 5 minutes. Season to taste with salt and pepper. Set aside.

Place the dough in a large bowl and add the flour, melted
shortening or lard, baking powder and salt. Moisten your hands and
knead the dough in the bowl until it is soft but not sticky, about
5 minutes. Cover with a damp cloth and set aside for 10 minutes.

Following the directions for forming tortillas on pages 8–9, shape
the dough into 12 balls each about 1½ inches (4 cm) in diameter
and then press into tortillas about 5 inches (13 cm) in diameter.

Spread a spoonful of the mushroom filling on one half of each
tortilla, leaving a ½-inch (12-mm) border. Fold the uncovered
portion over the filling and press the edges together to seal.

In a large frying pan over medium heat, pour in oil to a depth of
½ inch (12 mm). When the oil is hot, slip in the tortillas, one or two
at a time, and fry, turning once, until golden, about 2 minutes on
each side. Using a slotted spoon, transfer to paper towels to drain.
Serve immediately.

Makes 12 quesadillas

Ceviche with Shrimp
CEVICHE CON CAMARONES

1 lb (500 g) cooked shrimp, peeled and
  deveined

1 lb (500 g) mackerel, sea bass or red
  snapper fillets, cut into ½-inch (12-mm)
  cubes

2 cups (16 fl oz/500 ml) fresh lime juice

⅓ cup (3 fl oz/80 ml) olive oil

5 cloves garlic

2 lb (1 kg) ripe tomatoes

1 cup (4 oz/125 g) chopped onion

⅓ cup (⅓ oz/10 g) finely chopped fresh
  cilantro (fresh coriander)

½ cup (4 fl oz/125 ml) ketchup

2 tablespoons bottled mild red chili sauce,
  red picante salsa *(recipe on page 12)* or
  red molcajete salsa *(page 13)* (optional)

1 tablespoon dried oregano, crumbled

½ teaspoon salt

¼ teaspoon freshly ground black pepper

2 tablespoons finely chopped canned
  pickled serrano or jalapeño chili pepper

⅔ cup (4 oz/125 g) chopped green olives,
  plus whole green olives for garnish
  (optional)

1 tablespoon well-drained capers, finely
  chopped

2 ripe avocados, halved, pitted, peeled and
  coarsely chopped (optional)

The lime juice marinade turns the raw seafood firm and opaque, as if it were cooked, in this refreshing appetizer, which is also good as a light luncheon course. If you feel uneasy about marinating the fish at room temperature, cover it with plastic wrap and refrigerate for 4–5 hours, twice the normal preparation time. You can use almost any seafood, including scallops, oysters and precooked octopus; if a ceviche includes all these choices it becomes a dish known as vuelve a la vida, "return to life," a popular restorative all over Mexico. Serve the ceviche with crackers, crusty French bread and white wine.

Place the shrimp and fish in a glass bowl and pour the lime juice over them. Cover and let stand at room temperature for 2½ hours.

In a small frying pan over medium heat, warm the olive oil. Add the garlic cloves and sauté for 2–3 minutes, to flavor the oil. Discard the garlic. Let the oil cool completely.

Cut the tomatoes in half crosswise and gently squeeze out the seeds. Chop the tomatoes, being careful not to lose any of their juices, and place in a large bowl. Add the onion, cilantro, ketchup, chili sauce or salsa (if using), oregano, salt, black pepper, chilies, chopped olives, capers and cooled oil. Stir to mix well.

Remove the shrimp and fish from the lime juice and rinse a few times with cold water to remove excess lime juice. Add the shrimp and fish to the tomato mixture and toss to combine. Taste and adjust the seasonings.

Cover and chill before serving, but for no longer than 2 hours. Garnish with the avocado and whole olives, if desired.

Serves 6–8

Melted Cheese with Mushrooms and Chorizo

Queso Fundido con Champiñones y Chorizo

1 small Mexican chorizo sausage, ¼ lb
   (120 g), skinned and crumbled
1 tablespoon unsalted butter
3 oz (90 g) fresh mushrooms, cut into
   slices ¼ inch (6 mm) thick (about 1 cup)
salt and freshly ground pepper
2 cups (8 oz/250 g) shredded mild
   Cheddar or Monterey jack cheese
12 flour tortillas, heated
fresh Mexican salsa or tomatillo salsa
   (recipes on pages 12–13)

Especially popular in Mexico's northern states, this appetizer is traditionally cooked on top of the stove in cazuelitas—little clay pottery casseroles. The melted cheese mixture is then folded into warm flour tortillas with salsa. Less conventionally, it could also be served as a dip for crisp totopos (recipe on page 9).

Preheat an oven to 400°F (200°C).

   In a frying pan over medium-high heat, fry the crumbled chorizo until the fat is rendered and the sausage is slightly crisp, 6–8 minutes. Remove from the heat, cover and keep warm.

   In a frying pan over medium heat, melt the butter. Add the mushrooms and sauté until just tender, 2–3 minutes. Season to taste with salt and pepper. Remove from the heat, cover and keep warm.

   Lightly grease 2 small baking dishes. Divide the cheese evenly between the dishes. Add half of the mushrooms to one dish and half of the chorizo to the other dish. Bake until the cheese is melted and bubbling, 8–10 minutes.

   Add the remaining mushrooms and chorizo to each dish and serve hot with flour tortillas and salsa. Each guest spoons some of the melted cheese mixture into the center of a tortilla, adds salsa to taste, folds the tortilla in half and eats it out of hand.

Serves 6

Tomato–Pumpkin Seed Dip

Zicil-p'ak

1 cup (5 oz/140 g) hulled raw pumpkin
seeds

1 fresh habanero, serrano or jalapeño chili
pepper

2 ripe tomatoes

2 cloves garlic

2 tablespoons finely chopped onion

3 tablespoons chopped fresh cilantro
(fresh coriander)

salt

Marilyn Tausend, a Seattle food writer who has a great knowledge of Mexican cuisine, supplied the recipe for this spicy Yucatán dip, which takes its name from the Mayan words for the two main ingredients, pumpkin seeds and tomatoes. Be aware that a habanero chili has a much hotter taste than either the jalapeño or serrano. Hulled raw (untoasted) pumpkin seeds are widely available in health-food stores. Serve the dip with totopos (recipe on page 9), raw vegetables, toasted bread wedges, or crackers. It can be covered and stored in the refrigerator for up to 24 hours.

*I*n a dry, heavy frying pan over low heat, toast the pumpkin seeds, shaking the pan occasionally, until lightly browned, about 8 minutes; watch carefully that they do not burn. Remove the seeds and set aside.

In the same pan over medium heat, place the chili, tomatoes and garlic. Roast, turning occasionally, until well charred, about 4 minutes for the chili and tomatoes and 3 minutes for the garlic. Remove from the heat, cover and set aside to cool. Alternatively, place the chili and tomatoes in a closed paper bag to cool.

Place the toasted pumpkin seeds in a molcajete, if available, or in a spice mill or mini blender and grind to a coarse powder.

Peel the tomatoes, coarsely chop and place in a blender or in a food processor fitted with the metal blade. Add the garlic and process for a few seconds until smooth. Transfer to a serving bowl and stir in the ground pumpkin seeds.

Peel the chili and cut in half. Remove the stem and ribs; if a milder dip is desired, remove the seeds as well. Chop the chili finely and add it, along with the onion and cilantro, to the tomato–pumpkin seed mixture. Season to taste with salt. Stir well and serve.

Makes about 1½ cups (12 fl oz/375 ml)

Tortilla Soup
SOPA DE TORTILLA

2 cloves garlic

½ onion, cut in half

4 ripe tomatoes

6 cups (48 fl oz/1.5 l) chicken stock

1 tablespoon corn oil or other vegetable oil, plus oil for frying

2 small fresh epazote or cilantro (fresh coriander) sprigs

salt and freshly ground pepper

8 corn tortillas

2 fresh pasilla chili peppers, cut into rings ½ inch (12 mm) wide and seeds removed

2 ripe avocados, halved, pitted, peeled and thinly sliced lengthwise

1 cup (5 oz/155 g) crumbled *queso fresco* or feta cheese

½ cup (4 fl oz/125 ml) thick sour cream (*see glossary*)

3 limes, halved

This classic soup—in a version served at Las Mañanitas restaurant in Cuernavaca—makes a hearty first course or light lunch. It is also an excellent way to use up day-old tortillas.

Heat a dry, heavy frying pan or a griddle over medium heat. Place the garlic, onion and tomatoes on the pan or griddle and roast, turning occasionally, until well charred, about 3 minutes for the garlic and onion and 4 minutes for the tomatoes. Remove from the heat. Peel the tomatoes, coarsely chop and place in a blender or in a food processor fitted with the metal blade. Add the garlic and onion and purée to form a smooth, thick purée, adding ¼ cup (2 fl oz/60 ml) of the chicken stock if the mixture is too thick.

In a large saucepan over high heat, warm the 1 tablespoon oil. Add the tomato purée and cook, stirring, for 2 minutes. Reduce the heat to low and cook, uncovered, until the purée thickens and reduces slightly, about 5 minutes longer. Add the epazote or cilantro and the remaining chicken stock and season to taste with salt and pepper. Cover and simmer for 15 minutes longer.

Meanwhile, cut the tortillas in half, then cut each half crosswise into thin strips. In a small frying pan over high heat, pour in oil to a depth of ½ inch (12 mm). When hot, working in batches, fry the tortilla pieces until crisp, about 3 minutes. Using a slotted spoon, transfer to paper towels to drain. Fry the chili rings in the same oil until crisp, about 1 minute. Transfer to paper towels to drain.

Add the fried tortilla strips to the simmering soup and ladle into 6 individual bowls. Top with some of the chili rings and avocado slices and sprinkle with the cheese. Offer the cream, limes and the remaining avocado slices and chili rings in separate bowls on the side. Serve immediately.

Serves 6

Butterflied Shrimp

Camarones Rasurados

¼ onion
1 bay leaf
salt
30 large shrimp (prawns)
1 onion, finely chopped
3 fresh jalapeño or serrano chili peppers,
   finely chopped
1 cup (8 fl oz/250 ml) fresh lime juice
6 tablespoons (3 fl oz/90 ml) olive oil
6 tablespoons (3 fl oz/90 ml) soy sauce
6 tablespoons (3 fl oz/90 ml) Worcestershire sauce
freshly ground pepper

The literal translation of the name of this quick-to-assemble recipe is "shaved shrimp," referring not only to the fact that the shrimp are deftly cut in halves lengthwise but also to the razor-sharp flavor of their accompanying sauce. The shrimp can also be cut into pieces, mixed with the onion, chilies, lime juice, olive oil, soy sauce, Worcestershire sauce, and salt and pepper and then mounded in peeled avocado halves. Rolls, crusty breads or salted crackers are good accompaniments to both the butterflied shrimp and the avocado version. Pour a brisk white wine.

Fill a large saucepan three-fourths full with water. Bring to a boil and add the ¼ onion, the bay leaf, salt to taste and the shrimp. Boil the shrimp until they turn pink and curl loosely, 3–5 minutes. Drain well, immerse in cold water to cool completely and drain again.

Peel each shrimp, then devein by making a lengthwise slit along the outside curve and removing the dark intestinal vein. To butterfly the shrimp, deepen the slit, but do not cut all the way through, and open the shrimp so it lays flat.

Arrange 5 butterflied shrimp on each of 6 individual plates. Sprinkle each serving with an equal amount of the chopped onion, chilies, lime juice, olive oil, soy sauce and Worcestershire sauce. Season to taste with pepper and serve.

Serves 6

Vegetable Quesadillas
Quesadillas de Verduras

1¼ teaspoons salt

1 cup (6 oz/185 g) fresh corn kernels

1 cup (5 oz/155 g) finely chopped green
beans

1 cup (5 oz/155 g) finely chopped carrot

1 cup (5 oz/155 g) finely chopped
zucchini (courgette)

4 tablespoons coarsely chopped fresh
epazote or cilantro (fresh coriander)

2 fresh serrano chili peppers, finely
chopped

⅔ cup (3 oz/90 g) freshly grated
Parmesan, pecorino romano or other
firm, dry cheese

1 lb (500 g) dough for corn tortillas
(recipe on page 9)

3 tablespoons all-purpose (plain) flour

corn oil or other vegetable oil for frying

1 cup (8 fl oz/250 ml) tomatillo salsa
(recipe on page 13)

6 romaine lettuce leaves, finely shredded

3 radishes, thinly sliced

½ cup (2½ oz/75 g) crumbled feta cheese,
optional

Filled with a mixture of fresh vegetables, these tortilla pockets are a specialty of the street markets in Chilapa, Guerrero. Parmesan or pecorino romano cheese is used here in place of the traditional Mexican queso fresco. Instead of being offered as an appetizer or snack, two or three of them may be served with rice and beans to make a light lunch.

*F*ill a saucepan three-fourths full with water and add 1 teaspoon of the salt. Bring to a boil and add the corn, green beans, carrot and zucchini. Cook, uncovered, until the vegetables are tender-crisp, 3–4 minutes. Drain well. Place in a bowl. Add the epazote or cilantro, chilies and grated cheese; stir well. Cover to keep warm.

Place the dough in a bowl and, with your fingers, work in the flour and the remaining ¼ teaspoon salt. The dough should be soft. If it is too dry, work in 1–2 tablespoons lukewarm water.

Following the directions for forming tortillas on pages 8–9, shape the dough into 12 balls each about 1½ inches (4 cm) in diameter and then press into tortillas about 5 inches (12 cm) in diameter.

Place an equal amount of the vegetable mixture atop one half of each tortilla, leaving a ½-inch (12-mm) border. Fold the uncovered portion over the filling and press the edges together well.

In a large frying pan over medium-high heat, pour in oil to a depth of ½ inch (12 mm). When the oil is hot, slip the filled tortillas, one or two at a time, into the oil and fry, turning once, until golden, about 2 minutes on each side. Using a slotted spoon, transfer to paper towels to drain.

Serve immediately. Top with the salsa, shredded lettuce, radishes and then the crumbled cheese, if desired.

Makes 12 quesadillas

Grilled Cheese Tortilla "Sandwiches"

SINCRONIZADAS

2 teaspoons unsalted butter
1 cup (3 oz/90 g) sliced fresh mushrooms
12 flour tortillas
1 lb (480 g) Cheddar cheese, shredded
3 fresh poblano chili peppers, about 7 oz
   (220 g) total weight, roasted, peeled and
   cut into long, thin strips (see glossary)
guacamole (recipe on page 25)
fresh Mexican salsa (recipe on page 12)

Perhaps the Mexican name for this dish comes from the fact that two tortillas are perfectly aligned—that is, synchronized—in each sandwichlike stack of melted Cheddar, mushrooms and roasted peppers. Or maybe it describes the ease and speed with which so many are prepared. Serve with refried beans (recipe on page 11).

*I*n a frying pan over medium heat, melt the butter. Add the mushrooms and sauté until tender, 3–5 minutes. Remove from the heat.

In a nonstick frying pan over medium heat, place a tortilla and top with one-sixth each of the cheese, sautéed mushrooms and chilies. Top with a second tortilla and press down slightly. Cook until the cheese melts and the bottom is lightly browned, about 2 minutes. Turn the "sandwich" over and cook on the second side until golden, about 1 minute.

Remove from the pan and repeat with the remaining ingredients. Cut each sandwich in half or quarters. Serve immediately with guacamole and salsa in separate bowls on the side.

Serves 6

Scrambled Egg Enchiladas
ENCHILADAS ROBERTO

2½ lb (1.25 kg) large ripe tomatoes
1 or 2 fresh jalapeño or serrano chili
  peppers, seeded if desired
¼ white onion, cut up, plus 1 tablespoon
  minced onion
1 clove garlic
1 tablespoon salt
7 tablespoons (3½ fl oz/105 ml) corn oil
  or other vegetable oil
12 corn tortillas
6 eggs, lightly beaten
½ cup (4 fl oz/125 ml) thick sour cream
  (*see glossary*)
⅔ cup (3½ oz/100 g) crumbled *queso*
  fresco or feta cheese
4 lettuce leaves, shredded
red (Spanish) onion rings

My father, Acapulco lawyer Roberto Palazuelos, invented this alternative to enchiladas filled with meat or cheese. Accompany with black pot beans (recipe on page 11) and guacamole (page 25) at brunch or lunchtime.

*P*lace the tomatoes in a saucepan over high heat and add water to cover. Bring to a boil and remove from the heat. Drain well. Peel the tomatoes, coarsely chop and place in a blender or in a food processor fitted with the metal blade. Add the chilies, cut-up onion, garlic and salt and process to form a smooth purée.

In a saucepan over medium heat, warm 1 tablespoon of the oil. Add the purée and cook, uncovered, until thickened, about 10 minutes. Cover and keep hot.

Heat the remaining 6 tablespoons (3 fl oz/90 ml) oil in a frying pan over high heat. Add the tortillas, one at a time, and fry to soften, a few seconds on each side. Using tongs, transfer to paper towels to drain, then stack and cover to keep warm.

Reduce the heat to medium and add the 1 tablespoon minced onion to the oil remaining in the pan. Sauté until slightly translucent, about 30 seconds. Add the beaten eggs and cook, stirring frequently, until done but not too dry.

Place an equal amount of the egg mixture on each tortilla, roll up into a cylinder and place on a platter. Cover with the warm tomato sauce. Pour the cream over the top and then sprinkle with the cheese and lettuce. Garnish with the red onion rings and serve immediately.

Serves 6

Steak Sandwiches

PEPITOS

2 cups (16 fl oz/500 ml) refried black
  beans *(recipe on page 11)*
1½ lb (750 g) beef tenderloin
salt and freshly ground pepper
3 tablespoons unsalted butter
1 tablespoon vegetable oil
12 small round French rolls, about
  5 inches (13 cm) in diameter, split
  horizontally
6 romaine lettuce leaves
2 ripe tomatoes, each cut into 6 slices
3 avocados, halved, pitted, peeled and
  thinly sliced
10 oz (300 g) onions, thinly sliced

Someone named "Little Pepe" is immortalized in the Spanish name for these classic steak sandwiches, popular at lunchtime all over Mexico. The steaks and rolls are also delicious grilled over a charcoal fire. You can substitute baguettes cut into 6-inch (15-cm) lengths for the rolls.

Place the refried beans in a saucepan over low heat. Add a little water if necessary to make a thick paste. Cook uncovered, stirring often, until heated through, about 5 minutes. Cover and keep warm over low heat.

Cut the beef tenderloin into 12 equal pieces. Using a meat pounder, gently pound the pieces until they are ¼ inch (6 mm) thick. Season to taste with salt and pepper.

In a large frying pan or griddle over high heat, melt 1 tablespoon of the butter with the oil. Add the beef and fry, turning once, until done to your liking, about 2 minutes on each side for medium-rare. Remove from the heat and cover to keep warm.

Spread the cut sides of the rolls with the remaining 2 tablespoons butter. In a frying pan over medium heat, place the rolls, buttered side down, and toast lightly, 1–2 minutes.

Spread about 1 tablespoon bean purée on the toasted side of one-half of each roll. Top with the meat. Cover with the top half, toasted side in. Place the sandwiches on individual plates, 2 on each plate. Arrange the lettuce leaves, tomatoes, avocado and onion on a large platter. Place the remaining bean purée in a bowl on the side. Diners garnish their own sandwiches.

Makes 12 sandwiches; serves 6

Ranch-Style Chilaquiles

CHILAQUILES DE RANCHO

vegetable oil for frying

15 corn tortillas, cut into 2-inch (5-cm) wedges

1 cup (8 fl oz/250 ml) tomato purée

1 onion, coarsely chopped, plus ½ onion, finely chopped

3 fresh poblano chili peppers, roasted, peeled and cut into long, thin strips (*see glossary*)

salt and freshly ground pepper

⅔ cup (3½ oz/100 g) crumbled *queso fresco* or feta cheese

1 cup (8 fl oz/250 ml) thick sour cream (*see glossary*)

Strips of poblano chili enhance the tangy tomato sauce that accompanies this favorite Mexican brunch dish. The recipe is a popular way to use up day-old tortillas, although it can also be made with fresh ones. Serve with refried beans (recipe on page 11) and eggs scrambled with chilies and tomatoes, and brew your favorite type of coffee.

In a frying pan over high heat, pour in oil to a depth of about 1½ inches (4 cm). When the oil is hot, working in batches, add the tortilla wedges and fry until slightly crisp, about 1 minute. Using a slotted spoon, transfer to paper towels to drain. Reserve the oil in the pan.

In a blender or in a food processor fitted with the metal blade, combine the tomato purée and the coarsely chopped onion. Process until smooth.

Reheat the oil over medium heat. Add the tomato-onion purée and fry for about 2 minutes. Add the chili strips and simmer until the sauce thickens, about 10 minutes. Season to taste with salt and pepper. Add the fried tortilla wedges to the simmering sauce and cook, uncovered, until the tortillas have softened and absorbed some of the sauce, a few minutes longer.

Transfer to a serving dish and top with the finely chopped onion, cheese and cream. Serve hot.

Serves 6–8

8–10 ears of corn, husks intact
about ⅓ cup (3 fl oz/80 ml) milk
½ teaspoon salt
2 tablespoons unsalted butter, at room
    temperature
1 cup (8 fl oz/250 ml) thick sour cream
    (*see glossary*)
salsa of choice (*recipes on pages 12–13*)
crumbled *queso fresco* or feta cheese,
    optional

Fresh Corn Tamales

UCHEPOS

You'll be surprised by the smooth, rich flavor of these buttery tamales from Michoacán. It is essential to use only the freshest corn. Accompany with beans or a green salad.

Remove the husks in large pieces and pick the silks from the corn. Wash the husks, dry them well and set aside.

Using a sharp knife, cut the kernels from the cobs; you should have about 5 cups (30 oz/900 g). Using a blender or a food processor fitted with the metal blade, process the kernels, 1 cup (6 oz/185 g) at a time, at high speed, gradually adding the milk to ease the processing. The corn should have the consistency of cottage cheese. Place in a bowl, add the salt and butter and stir to mix well.

Fill a large pan with hot water to a depth of 2–3 inches (5–7.5 cm). Line a steamer basket with the stiffest corn husks. Reserve 14–16 softer husks to use as wrappers.

On each soft husk, place a heaping spoonful of corn filling in the center. Fold the sides in loosely, overlapping them, and fold the bottom end over to rest atop the seam. The top end stays open. Layer, seam side up, in the basket. Cover with a layer of stiff husks.

Bring the water to a simmer. Cover and cook the tamales until the filling is firm (check by opening a tamale), about 1 hour. Check the water from time to time and add boiling water as needed to maintain original level. Remove from the heat and let cool for about 20 minutes, so the filling will not stick to the husks.

Serve the tamales in their husks. Accompany with separate bowls of the cream, salsa and cheese (if desired). Alternatively, open the tamales and top with cream, salsa and cheese before serving.

Makes 14–16 tamales; serves 4

Tuna-and-Avocado-Stuffed Poblano Chilies

CHILES POBLANOS RELLENOS CON ATÚN Y AGUACATE

12 fresh poblano chili peppers

FOR THE VINAIGRETTE:

1 cup (8 fl oz/250 ml) apple cider vinegar
1½ cups (12 fl oz/375 ml) olive oil
¼ teaspoon freshly ground pepper
2 teaspoons dried oregano, crumbled
2 lb (1 kg) red (Spanish) onions, thinly
  sliced

FOR THE FILLING:

2 cans (6½ oz/200 g each) tuna packed in
  oil or water, well drained
2 teaspoons finely chopped white onion
2 ripe avocados, halved, pitted, peeled and
  coarsely chopped, plus 2 additional
  avocados for garnish, optional
2 cups (6 oz/185 g) finely chopped
  romaine lettuce, plus 12 romaine or
  other lettuce leaves for garnish, optional
salt
2 teaspoons olive oil
2 teaspoons apple cider vinegar

Poblano chilies are commonly stuffed with all kinds of ingredients. In this light luncheon course, they are filled with a mixture of canned tuna and avocado, then marinated for a day in a brisk vinaigrette dressing that brings out their flavors. The recipe comes from Rosario Madero, a wonderful cook and the niece of Francisco I. Madero, Mexico's president from 1911 to 1913.

Roast and peel the chilies (see glossary), then slit lengthwise along one side and remove the ribs; leave stems intact. Set aside.

To make the vinaigrette, in a bowl whisk together the vinegar, olive oil, pepper and oregano. Add the sliced onion and stir gently to mix well.

To make the filling, in a bowl combine the tuna, chopped onion, chopped avocado, chopped lettuce, salt to taste, olive oil and vinegar. Stir together just until blended.

Divide the filling equally among the 12 chilies, stuffing it in gently so as not to tear them, and place the chilies in a single layer in a glass dish. Evenly distribute the vinaigrette-onion mixture over the top, cover and refrigerate for 24 hours.

Serve chilled. Garnish the dish with the lettuce leaves, if desired. If you like, pit, peel and slice 2 avocados lengthwise and garnish with the slices as well.

Serves 6

Tex-Mex Taco Salad

ENSALADA A LA TEJANA

1½ lb (750 g) ripe tomatoes (about 6),
    coarsely chopped, plus 2 ripe tomatoes,
    sliced
1 clove garlic
1 teaspoon salt
freshly ground pepper
1 tablespoon vegetable oil
1 lb (500 g) lean ground (minced) beef
1 large white onion, chopped
1 tablespoon chili powder
½ teaspoon ground cumin
½ teaspoon dried oregano, crumbled
6 cups (18 oz/560 g) shredded iceberg or
    romaine lettuce
1 cup (3 oz/90 g) sliced green (spring)
    onions, including green tops
1 cup (5 oz/155 g) peeled, seeded and
    diced cucumber
6 oz (185 g) sharp Cheddar cheese, cut
    into small cubes (about 1½ cups)
3 cups (9 oz/280 g) crushed tortilla chips
    or *totopos* (recipe on page 9)

Think of this Mexican-influenced north-of-the-border favorite as a sort of tossed tostada or taco-in-a-salad-bowl. Feel free to substitute chicken or pork for the beef.

In a blender or in a food processor fitted with the metal blade, combine the chopped tomatoes, garlic, salt and pepper to taste. Process to form a smooth purée.

In a small frying pan over medium heat, warm the oil. Add the tomato purée and cook uncovered, stirring often, until thickened, about 10 minutes. Remove from the heat and let cool completely.

In a frying pan over medium-high heat, crumble in the beef and fry, stirring, until cooked, just a few minutes. Stir in the white onion and cook, continuing to stir, until soft, about 10 minutes. Pour off any excess fat and stir in the chili powder, cumin, oregano and 3 heaping tablespoons of the tomato sauce. Mix well.

In a large salad bowl, combine the lettuce, green onions, cucumber, cheese and the warm beef mixture. Mix well. Sprinkle with the crushed tortilla chips and top with the tomato slices. Serve at once with the remaining tomato sauce in a bowl alongside for diners to add to taste.

Serves 6–8

Cheese Crêpes with Guajillo Chili Sauce

CREPAS DE QUESO CON SALSA DE CHILE GUAJILLO

3½ oz (100 g) dried guajillo chili peppers

1 egg

1 cup (8 fl oz/250 ml) milk

½ cup (2½ oz/75 g) all-purpose (plain) flour

1 teaspoon plus 1 tablespoon corn oil or other vegetable oil

butter for cooking crêpes

2 tablespoons canned beef consommé or 1 bouillon cube dissolved in 1 tablespoon hot water

2 tablespoons Maggi sauce

2 cloves garlic

2 tablespoons chopped onion

2 tablespoons salt

¼ teaspoon freshly ground pepper

1 cup (4 oz/125 g) shredded Cheddar cheese

½ cup (4 fl oz/125 ml) thick sour cream (*see glossary*)

Guajillo chilies impart a subtle flavor to these luncheon crêpes.

Slit the chilies lengthwise along one side and remove the seeds, ribs and stems. In a dry, heavy frying pan over low heat, toast the chilies until they deepen in color, about 3 minutes. Transfer to a bowl and add lukewarm water to cover; let stand for 5 minutes, then drain. Set aside.

In a blender combine the egg, milk, flour and the 1 teaspoon oil. Process until the mixture is smooth, about 30 seconds. Place a nonstick crêpe pan or small frying pan over medium-low heat (or use 2 pans). Lightly grease with butter and then pour in 3 tablespoons batter. Quickly rotate the pan to coat the bottom thinly. Cook until the edges are dry, about 30 seconds; turn and cook on the second side until lightly golden, about 15 seconds. The crêpe should be pliable. Transfer to a plate and repeat with the remaining batter, stacking the crêpes. Cover to keep warm. You should have 12 crêpes in all, each about 5 inches (13 cm) in diameter.

Rinse the blender container, then combine in it the softened chilies, beef consommé or dissolved bouillon cube, Maggi sauce, garlic, onion, salt and pepper. Process until smooth.

Preheat an oven to 400°F (200°C). In a saucepan over high heat, warm the 1 tablespoon oil. Add the chili purée and cook, uncovered, until the sauce thickens slightly, about 10 minutes.

Grease a 9-inch (23-cm) square baking dish. Place 1 heaping tablespoon of the cheese on each crêpe, roll up into cylinders and place seam-side down in the prepared dish. Cover with the chili mixture and bake until bubbling, about 20 minutes. Pour the cream over the top and serve hot.

Serves 6

Oven-Crisped Burritos with Shredded Pork

CHIMICHANGAS CON CARNE DE PUERCO DESHEBRADA

1½ lb (750 g) lean pork, cut into 2-inch (5-cm) chunks

3 cups (24 fl oz/750 ml) hot water

3 tablespoons distilled white vinegar

¼ cup (1½ oz/45 g) finely chopped canned green chili peppers

1 clove garlic

½ teaspoon dried oregano, crumbled

½ teaspoon ground cumin

salt

8 flour tortillas, each 8 inches (20 cm) in diameter

¼ cup (2 oz/60 g) unsalted butter or margarine, melted

2 cups (8 oz/250 g) shredded Cheddar or Monterey jack cheese

1 cup (8 fl oz/250 ml) thick sour cream *(see glossary)*

red picante, red molcajete, tomatillo or fresh Mexican salsa *(recipes on pages 12–13)*

guacamole *(recipe on page 25)*

Linguists continue to debate the exact meaning of the word chimichanga, *which refers to a crisp north-of-the-border burrito that probably originated in Tucson, Arizona. In this version, the burritos are baked rather than fried, for lighter results. Beef, lamb, turkey or chicken may be substituted for the pork.*

In a large, dry frying pan over medium-high heat, brown the pork on all sides, 8–10 minutes. Add the hot water, stirring the pan bottom to loosen any browned bits, and bring to a boil. Reduce the heat to low, cover and simmer until the meat is tender, about 1¼ hours.

Preheat an oven to 450°F (230°C). Uncover the frying pan, raise the heat to high and boil to evaporate all of the water. Reduce the heat to medium and add the vinegar, chilies, garlic, oregano and cumin. Stir well and remove from the heat. Let cool completely. Using your fingers or 2 forks, shred the meat. Season with salt.

Brush both sides of each tortilla with melted butter or margarine. Place an equal amount of the pork mixture on the center of each tortilla. Fold in the sides, overlapping them, then fold over the ends to rest atop the seam. Place seam-side down on a baking sheet.

Bake until golden, 8–10 minutes. Serve immediately. Accompany with the cheese, cream, salsa and guacamole in separate bowls on the side for spooning on top.

Makes 8 burritos; serves 4

Crab Meat Tostadas

TOSTADAS DE JAIBA

corn oil or other vegetable oil for frying
12 corn tortillas
½ lb (250 g) fresh or canned crab meat,
  picked over to remove bits of shell and
  cartilage
2 cups (12 oz/375 g) chopped tomatoes
1 cup (4 oz/125 g) chopped onion
½ cup (¾ oz/20 g) finely chopped fresh
  cilantro (fresh coriander)
2 tablespoons olive oil
1 tablespoon finely chopped canned
  pickled jalapeño chili pepper, plus
  2½ tablespoons liquid from can
1 tablespoon dried oregano, crumbled
¼ cup (2 fl oz/60 ml) fresh lemon juice
1¼ teaspoons salt
2 ripe avocados, halved, pitted, peeled
  and chopped

You'll find crab in abundance in Tampico, the city on Mexico's Gulf coast where this light dish originates. If you like, substitute ceviche (recipe on page 33) or cooked shrimp (prawns) for the crab meat. Serve with white wine or beer.

In a frying pan over high heat, pour in oil to a depth of ½ inch (12 mm). Add the tortillas, one at a time, and fry, turning once, until crisp and golden, 45–60 seconds on each side. Using tongs, transfer to paper towels to drain. (The tortillas can be fried up to 1 hour before assembling the tostadas.)

Using a fork, flake the crab meat into a bowl. Add the tomatoes, onion, cilantro, olive oil, chopped chili, chili liquid, oregano, lemon juice and salt. Mix lightly.

Place 2 fried tortillas on each individual plate. Place a heaping spoonful of the crab meat mixture on each tortilla and top with the avocado. Serve immediately.

Makes 12 tostadas; serves 6

Carmelo's Tuna Tacos au Gratin
TACOS DE ATÚN GRATINADOS

4 cloves garlic, minced

1 onion, about 3½ oz (100 g), coarsely
chopped, plus ½ onion, sliced

1 lb (500 g) ripe tomatoes, coarsely
chopped, plus 2 ripe tomatoes, thinly
sliced

3 fresh serrano chili peppers, coarsely
chopped

3 cups (24 fl oz/750 ml) water

1 teaspoon salt

½ teaspoon Worcestershire sauce

¼ teaspoon soy sauce

1 tablespoon corn oil or other vegetable
oil, plus oil for frying

18 corn tortillas

2 cans (6½ oz/200 g each) tuna packed in
oil or water, drained and flaked

1½ cups (6 oz/180 g) shredded Cheddar
cheese

Chef Carmelo Berru at Club Deportivo de Las Brisas in Acapulco devised this remarkably simple dish. Serve with pot beans or refried beans (recipes on page 11), a mixed green salad and guacamole (page 25).

In a blender or in a food processor fitted with the metal blade, combine the garlic, chopped onion, chopped tomato, chilies, water, salt, Worcestershire and soy sauce. Process until smooth, about 30 seconds. Set aside.

In a saucepan over medium heat, warm the 1 tablespoon oil. Add the sliced onion and sauté until limp, about 2 minutes. Add the purée and cook, uncovered, over medium heat until thickened, about 15 minutes. Set aside and cover to keep warm.

To make the tacos, place a large spoonful of tuna on each tortilla (warm them if necessary to make them more pliable; see pages 8–9) and roll up into a cylinder. Secure 2 or 3 tacos together, seam sides in, with 1 or 2 toothpicks, running them through the center.

In a frying pan over high heat, pour in oil to a depth of 1 inch (2.5 cm). When hot, working in batches, fry the tacos until golden but not too crisp, about 5 minutes. Using a slotted spoon, transfer to paper towels to drain; remove the toothpicks.

Return the pan with the sauce to low heat. Add the tacos and simmer until they soften and the sauce thickens, about 6 minutes.

Meanwhile, preheat a broiler (griller). Place 3 tacos on each of 6 flameproof plates and spoon the sauce over the top. Divide the tomato slices and then the cheese among the servings. Slip under the broiler and broil (grill) until the cheese melts, about 2 minutes. Alternatively, place in a microwave set on high for about 1 minute. Serve immediately.

Serves 6

Open-Faced Bean-and-Cheese Sandwiches

MOLLETES

6 French rolls, split horizontally
unsalted butter or margarine, optional
1 cup (8 fl oz/250 ml) refried pinto beans
  (recipe on page 11)
2 lb (1 kg) Cheddar cheese, thinly sliced
1 cup (8 fl oz/250 ml) fresh Mexican salsa
  (recipe on page 12)

Excellent as a luncheon or brunch dish, this popular Mexico City creation goes well with scrambled eggs or a simple green salad. Lengths of French bread may be substituted for the individual rolls. If you like, crumble cooked chorizo or other spicy sausage into the beans. The sandwiches can also be heated in a 375°F (190°C) oven for about 15 minutes. Coffee is traditionally sipped with the molletes.

Preheat a broiler (griller).

If you like, spread the cut sides of the rolls with butter or margarine. Then spread each with about 1 rounded table-spoon of the refried beans. Top with the cheese slices. Arrange on a broiler tray and slip under the broiler. Broil (grill) until the cheese melts. Serve immediately with the salsa.

Makes 12 sandwiches; serves 6

Chicken Tostadas

TOSTADAS DE POLLO

1 whole chicken breast or 2 breast halves

corn oil or other vegetable oil for frying

12 corn tortillas

1½ cups (12 fl oz/375 ml) refried beans
  (recipe on page 11)

1 Mexican chorizo or other spicy sausage,
  about ½ lb (250 g), skinned, crumbled
  and fried

3 cups (9 oz/280 g) shredded lettuce

1 onion, thinly sliced

2 ripe tomatoes, thinly sliced

1 ripe avocado, halved, pitted, peeled
  and sliced

salt

1 cup (8 fl oz/250 ml) thick sour cream
  (see glossary)

¾ cup (4 oz/125 g) crumbled *queso fresco*
  or feta cheese

fresh Mexican salsa or red molcajete salsa
  (recipes on pages 12–13)

Crisply fried corn tortillas form a base for layers of chicken, beans, sausage, lettuce, onion, tomato and avocado to make a popular casual luncheon dish served all over Mexico. You can substitute cooked turkey or pork for the chicken. For an hors d'oeuvre party, assemble bite-sized versions on tiny tortillas, as shown here.

Place the chicken in a saucepan with water to cover. Bring to a boil, reduce the heat to low, cover and simmer until tender, about 25 minutes. Drain well and let cool completely. Bone and skin the chicken, then, using your fingers or 2 forks, shred the meat. Set aside.

In a small frying pan over high heat, pour in oil to a depth of ½ inch (12 mm). Add the tortillas, one at a time, and fry, turning once, until crisp and golden, 45–60 seconds on each side. Using tongs, transfer to paper towels to drain. (The tortillas can be fried up to 1 hour before assembling the tostadas.)

In a small frying pan reheat the refried beans over low heat. If the beans seem too thick to spread, add a few teaspoons of water to thin slightly. Stir in the chorizo. Place 2 fried tortillas on each individual plate. Spread a spoonful of the hot bean mixture onto each tortilla. Top with a layer each of chicken, lettuce, onion, tomato and avocado. Season to taste with salt. Top with the cream and sprinkle with the cheese. Serve immediately with the salsa on the side.

Makes 12 tostadas; serves 6

Chicken Tacos in Broth

TACOS AHOGADOS

6 cups (48 fl oz/1.5 l) water

2 large whole chicken breasts or 4 breast halves

½ large onion

1 clove garlic

salt

36 corn tortillas

corn oil or other vegetable oil for frying

freshly ground pepper

1 head iceberg lettuce, cored and shredded

6 radishes, sliced

1 cup (8 fl oz/250 ml) thick sour cream (*see glossary*)

1 cup (4 oz/125 g) shredded Cheddar cheese

tomatillo salsa (*recipe on page 13*)

lime wedges

A popular dish from Acapulco, these "drowned tacos" make a nice luncheon course preceded by a simple salad and accompanied with lemonade or white wine. The tacos are picked up and eaten out of hand, and the soup is spooned from the bowl. Accompany with your favorite salsa (recipes on pages 12–13), for both dipping the tacos and seasoning the broth to taste. You can also add chicken livers to each bowl, precooked on the side in a little broth. Finely shredded cabbage makes another crisp and flavorful garnish.

*I*n a large saucepan over high heat, combine the water, chicken, onion, garlic and salt to taste. Bring to a boil, reduce the heat to low, cover and simmer until the chicken is tender, about 25 minutes. Remove from the heat and remove the chicken from the broth; strain the broth and return it to the pan. Let the chicken cool completely, then bone and skin. Using your fingers or 2 forks, shred the meat.

Place an equal amount of the chicken meat on each tortilla and roll up into a cylinder; secure in place with a toothpick. In a frying pan over high heat, pour in oil to a depth of ½ inch (12 mm). When the oil is hot, working in batches, add the filled tortillas and fry until golden, about 4 minutes. Using a slotted spoon or tongs, transfer to paper towels to drain; remove the toothpicks.

Season the reserved broth with salt and pepper and bring to a boil. Boil for a few seconds, then remove from the heat. Divide the broth among individual soup bowls. Put 3 tacos in each bowl and top with the lettuce and radishes. Serve the cream, cheese, salsa and lime wedges in separate bowls on the side, for diners to add to taste.

Serves 12

Crab Meat Tacos

TACOS CON RELLENO DE JAIBA

1 dried ancho chili pepper, seeded and deribbed
½ teaspoon ground cinnamon
¼ teaspoon coriander seeds
¼ teaspoon ground cumin
6 peppercorns
3 cloves garlic
½ cup (4 fl oz/125 ml) water
2 tablespoons corn oil or other vegetable oil
¾ cup (4½ oz/140 g) chopped, peeled tomato
½ onion, finely chopped
1 bell pepper (capsicum), seeded, deribbed and finely chopped
1 fresh jalapeño or serrano chili pepper, finely chopped
1 bay leaf
1 teaspoon well-drained capers, finely chopped
10 green olives, pitted and finely chopped, plus whole olives for garnish
1 lb (500 g) flaked, cooked crab meat, picked over to remove bits of shell and cartilage
½ cup (2½ oz/75 g) shredded carrot
salt
fresh cilantro (fresh coriander) sprigs for garnish
24 corn tortillas, warmed
1 cup (8 fl oz/250 ml) red picante salsa (recipe on page 12)

A spicy, quickly sautéed mixture of crab meat and vegetables is used here as a flavorful filling for soft tacos. Any other freshly cooked or leftover fish, broken up into shreds, may be substituted for the crab. Serve with white wine or fresh fruit drinks.

*P*lace the ancho chili in a small saucepan over high heat and add water to cover. Bring to a boil, reduce the heat to medium-low and simmer, uncovered, until the chili is soft, 4–5 minutes. Drain well.

In a blender or in a food processor fitted with the metal blade, combine the softened chili, cinnamon, coriander seeds, cumin, peppercorns, garlic and water. Process to form a smooth purée.

In a frying pan over medium heat, warm the oil. Add the tomato, onion, bell pepper, fresh chili, bay leaf, capers and chopped olives and sauté until soft, about 5 minutes. Add the ancho chili purée, stir well and simmer for a few minutes, to blend the flavors. Add the crab meat and carrot, stir well and heat to serving temperature. Season to taste with salt.

To serve, transfer to a shallow serving dish and garnish with whole olives and cilantro sprigs. Serve with the warm tortillas and salsa. Each diner spoons some of the crab mixture onto a tortilla and tops with salsa.

Serves 6–8

Shredded Beef Burritos
Burritos de Carne Deshebrada de Res

1 lb (500 g) boneless beef chuck, in one
  piece
3 cups (24 fl oz/750 ml) water
6 peppercorns
1 small onion
salt to taste, plus ¼ teaspoon salt
1 clove garlic
1 tablespoon vegetable oil
1 fresh poblano chili pepper, roasted,
  peeled and cut into long, thin strips
  (see glossary)
2 small tomatoes, peeled and finely
  chopped
¼ teaspoon ground cumin
freshly ground pepper
8 flour tortillas, each 8 inches (20 cm) in
  diameter
1 cup (8 fl oz/250 ml) refried beans
  (recipe on page 11)
1 cup (3 oz/90 g) shredded lettuce
red picante, red molcajete, tomatillo or
  fresh Mexican salsa (recipes on pages
  12–13)
guacamole (recipe on page 25)

*Assemble these generously stuffed flour tortillas just before serving, so the
tortillas don't get soggy. Pork or chicken may be substituted for the beef.*

*I*n a large saucepan over high heat, combine the meat, water,
peppercorns, ⅓ of the onion and salt to taste. Bring to a boil, reduce
the heat to low, cover and simmer until the meat is tender, about
1½ hours.

Transfer the beef to a plate. Strain the broth, reserving ⅓ cup
(3 fl oz/80 ml). Let the beef cool, then, using your fingers or 2 forks,
shred the meat.

Place the garlic in a mortar or in a small bowl with the ¼ teaspoon
salt. Using a pestle or the back of a spoon, mash to form a paste.

Chop the remaining ⅔ onion. In a large frying pan over medium
heat, warm the oil. Add the chopped onion and garlic paste and
sauté, stirring, until the onion is soft, about 2 minutes. Add the chili
strips and tomatoes and cook, stirring, until soft, 3–4 minutes. Add
the shredded meat, cumin and pepper to taste. Stir until the meat is
heated through. Add the reserved beef broth and season to taste
with salt. Cover to keep warm and set aside.

In a nonstick frying pan or griddle over medium heat, warm the
tortillas, turning once. Alternatively, enclose the tortillas in plastic
wrap and place in a microwave oven for about 30 seconds. Place the
refried beans in a heavy saucepan over medium heat and heat
through, adding water if needed to form a thick sauce.

Place some of the beef mixture on the center of each tortilla and
top with some of the refried beans and lettuce and then with salsa and
guacamole to taste. Fold in the sides, overlapping them, then fold
over the ends to rest atop the seam. Place seam-side down on individual plates or on a serving platter. Serve with extra salsa on the side.

Makes 8 burritos; serves 4

Vegetarian Burritos
Burritos Vegetarianos

2 tablespoons corn oil or other vegetable oil
1 large onion, finely chopped
2 large carrots, peeled and thinly sliced
1 clove garlic, minced
1 fresh jalapeño or serrano chili pepper, seeded, deribbed and finely chopped
1 teaspoon dried oregano, crumbled
½ teaspoon ground cumin
2 cups (10 oz/315 g) diced zucchini (courgette)
1 green or red bell pepper (capsicum), seeded, deribbed and chopped
1 cup (6 oz/185 g) fresh or frozen corn kernels
1 can (1 lb/500 g) kidney beans, drained
12 flour tortillas, each 8 inches (20 cm) in diameter
1 cup (8 fl oz/250 ml) thick sour cream (*see glossary*)
1 cup (4 oz/125 g) shredded Cheddar cheese
shredded lettuce
tomatillo salsa or fresh Mexican salsa (*recipes on pages 12–13*)

The term burrito, *which comes from the American Southwest, pays tribute to little burros—pack animals capable of carrying abundant cargo. That's an apt description for these generously filled flour tortillas, packed with seasoned fresh vegetables. By all means vary the vegetable mixture depending upon what is in season at your market.*

In a large frying pan over medium heat, warm the oil. Add the onion, carrots, garlic, chili, oregano and cumin and sauté until tender, about 10 minutes. Add the zucchini, bell pepper, corn and kidney beans and cook until the zucchini is tender-crisp, 6–8 minutes longer.

Warm a nonstick frying pan or griddle over medium heat and heat the tortillas, turning once. Alternatively, enclose the tortillas in plastic wrap and place in a microwave oven for about 30 seconds. Place an equal amount of the vegetable filling in the center of each tortilla. Fold in the sides, overlapping them, then fold over the ends to rest atop the seam.

Serve the burritos immediately. Accompany with the cream, cheese, shredded lettuce and salsa in separate bowls on the side for spooning over the top.

Makes 12 burritos; serves 6

Chicken Chilaquiles with Beer
CHILAQUILES CON CERVEZA Y POLLO

1 whole chicken breast or 2 breast halves
2 dried ancho chili peppers
corn oil or other vegetable oil for frying
12 corn tortillas, each cut into 6 wedges
2 ripe tomatoes, coarsely chopped
1 cup (8 fl oz/250 ml) beer
3 eggs
1 cup (8 fl oz/250 ml) thick sour cream
    (see glossary)
salt and freshly ground pepper
1⅔ cups (6½ oz/200 g) grated Cheddar
    cheese

This unusual variation on the popular brunch or luncheon dish (see page 50) combines shredded chicken with tortillas and a creamy sauce of tomatoes, beer and ancho chilies. Try leftover pork, beef or fish instead of the chicken, if you like.

Place the chicken in a saucepan with water to cover. Bring to a boil, reduce the heat to low, cover and simmer until tender, about 25 minutes. Drain well and let cool completely. Bone and skin the chicken, then, using your fingers or 2 forks, shred the meat. Set aside.

Meanwhile, slit the chilies lengthwise along one side and remove the ribs and stems. In a dry, heavy frying pan over low heat, toast the chilies until they deepen in color and smell quite pungent, about 3 minutes. Transfer to a bowl and add lukewarm water to cover; let stand for 5 minutes, then drain. Set aside.

Preheat an oven to 400°F (200°C).

In a large frying pan over high heat, pour in oil to a depth of 1½ inches (4 cm). When the oil is hot, working in batches, add the tortilla wedges and fry until slightly golden but not too crisp, about 1 minute. Using a slotted spoon, transfer to paper towels to drain.

Spread the fried tortilla wedges in a 9-by-12-by-3-inch (23-by-30-by-7.5-cm) baking dish. Top evenly with the shredded chicken.

Drain the chilies well and place in a food processor fitted with the metal blade or in a blender. Add the tomatoes, beer, eggs, cream and salt and pepper to taste. Process until smooth.

Pour the chili mixture evenly over the tortillas and chicken. Top with the cheese. Bake until the cheese melts and is bubbling, about 30 minutes. Serve immediately.

Serves 6

Tortillas in Bean Purée with Cheese

ENFRIJOLADAS RELLENAS DE QUESO

2 cups (16 fl oz/500 ml) pot beans made with black beans *(recipe on page 11)*

2 tablespoons corn oil or other vegetable oil, plus oil for frying

¼ white onion

salt

12 corn tortillas

½ cup (4 fl oz/125 ml) thick sour cream *(see glossary)*

¾ cup (4 oz/125 g) crumbled *queso fresco* or feta cheese

1 red (Spanish) onion, thinly sliced and separated into rings

½ cup (4 fl oz/125 ml) tomatillo salsa *(recipe on page 13)*

Among the simplest of tortilla preparations, this delicious dish makes a high-protein luncheon main course. If you like, fill the tortillas with scrambled eggs as well. Serve with salad and a choice of beer or fresh fruit drinks.

In a blender or in a food processor fitted with the metal blade, purée the beans until they are the consistency of a sauce, adding a little water if the purée is too thick.

In a frying pan over medium heat, warm the 2 tablespoons oil. Add the white onion and sauté until browned, about 2 minutes. Add the puréed beans, reduce the heat to low and cook uncovered, stirring often, for 2 minutes. It should have the consistency of a thin sauce. Discard the onion. Season the purée to taste with salt, cover and keep warm over low heat.

In another frying pan over high heat, pour in oil to a depth of ½ inch (12 mm). Add the tortillas, one at a time, and fry quickly, turning once, until softened, about 5 seconds on each side. Using tongs, transfer each tortilla to paper towels to drain briefly, then dip it in the hot bean sauce, fold it in half and transfer to individual plates, placing 2 tortillas on each plate.

Spoon additional bean purée over the top, then top with the cream and crumbled cheese. Garnish with the red onion rings and the tomatillo salsa.

Serves 6

Mexican Chicken Pie

PASTEL DEL POBRE

1 large whole chicken breast or 2 breast
  halves
½ lb (250 g) tomatillos, husks removed
5 fresh serrano chili peppers
¼ onion, cut up, plus 1 onion, thinly
  sliced
1 clove garlic
½ cup (¾ oz/20 g) chopped fresh cilantro
  (fresh coriander)
1 chicken bouillon cube, crushed
corn oil or other vegetable oil for frying
18 corn tortillas
½ lb (250 g) cooked ham, chopped
6 fresh poblano chili peppers, roasted,
  peeled and cut into long, thin strips
  (see glossary)
1 cup (8 fl oz/250 ml) thick sour cream
  (see glossary)
1 cup (4 oz/125 g) shredded Cheddar
  cheese

The Mexican name may translate literally as "poor man's pie," but there is nothing deprived about this simple but luxurious casserole. Try substituting leftover turkey for the chicken. Serve with a tossed green salad.

Place the chicken in a saucepan with water to cover. Bring to a boil, reduce the heat to low, cover and simmer until tender, about 25 minutes. Drain well and let cool completely. Bone and skin the chicken, then, using your fingers or 2 forks, shred the meat. Set aside.

In a dry, heavy frying pan or griddle over medium heat, roast the tomatillos and serrano chilies, turning occasionally, until well charred, 4–5 minutes. Remove from the heat; when cool enough to handle, stem the chilies.

In a blender or in a food processor fitted with the metal blade, combine the roasted tomatillos and serrano chilies, the ¼ onion, garlic, cilantro and bouillon cube. Purée until smooth. It should have the consistency of a cream soup; thin with water if needed.

Preheat an oven to 375°F (190°C). In a frying pan over high heat, pour in oil to a depth of ½ inch (12 mm). When hot, fry the tortillas, one at a time and turning once, just until softened, about 5 seconds per side. Using tongs, transfer to paper towels to drain.

In a shallow 9-by-12-inch (23-by-30-cm) baking dish, arrange 6 tortillas, overlapping them. Top evenly with the chicken and half of the tomatillo purée. Cover with 6 more tortillas and top evenly with the ham, poblano chili strips and onion slices. Pour on the remaining tomatillo purée and top with the remaining 6 tortillas. Pour the cream evenly over the surface. Sprinkle with the cheese.

Bake until the cheese melts and is bubbling, about 15 minutes. Cut into squares and serve.

Serves 6–8

Red Chicken Tamales

TAMALES DE POLLO ROJOS

2 whole chicken breasts or 4 breast halves

¼ onion, in one piece, plus ¼ onion, finely chopped

6 peppercorns

3 bay leaves

salt

4 fresh jalapeño chili peppers

¾ lb (375 g) tomatoes

1 clove garlic

1 tablespoon corn oil or other vegetable oil

¼ teaspoon cumin seeds

2 lb (1 kg) dough for corn tortillas (recipe on page 8)

½ cup (4 oz/125 g) lard or vegetable shortening, melted

30 dried corn husks, soaked in warm water for about 10 minutes until pliable, drained and dried

In a saucepan combine the chicken, ¼ onion, peppercorns, bay leaves, salt to taste and water to cover. Bring to a boil, reduce the heat to low, cover and simmer until tender, about 25 minutes. Remove the chicken; strain the broth, reserving ½ cup (4 fl oz/125 ml). Let the chicken cool, then bone and skin. Using your fingers or 2 forks, shred the meat. Set aside.

Fill a small saucepan three-fourths full with water and bring to a boil. Boil the chilies, uncovered, for 4 minutes. Add the tomatoes and boil for 2 minutes longer. Drain and stem them and place in a blender. Add the garlic and reserved stock and purée until smooth.

In a frying pan over medium heat, warm the oil. Add the chopped onion and cumin seeds and sauté until the onion is translucent, about 2 minutes. Add the tomato purée and cook over high heat until thickened, about 5 minutes. Add the chicken, reduce the heat to low and cook for 5 minutes to blend the flavors. Season to taste with salt. Thin with chicken stock, if necessary. Set aside.

In a bowl, using a fork or fingers, mix the tortilla dough and lard or shortening until soft. Set aside 10 corn husks. Place about 2 heaping tablespoons dough on the center of each of the remaining 20 husks. Flatten into a rectangle 2 by 3 inches (5 by 7.5 cm), with 1-inch (2.5-cm) border on all sides. Place about 1½ tablespoons chicken mixture on each rectangle. Starting from long side, roll up the husk, then fold the bottom over and the pointed tip down.

In a steamer pan pour in water to a depth of 2–3 inches (5–7.5 cm). Line the steamer rack with the reserved 10 husks and layer the tamales seam-side up in it. Place rack in steamer and bring to a boil. Cover and steam over low heat until dough does not stick to the husk (open a tamale to see if they are ready), about 1 hour. Add boiling water to pan as needed to maintain original level. Let stand for 20 minutes before serving. Serve hot.

Makes 20 tamales; serves 6–8

Fish and Tortilla Pie

PAN DE PESCADO

The layered combination of tortillas, tomato sauce, black beans and chunks of fish is a popular Lenten dish in the Yucatán.

✿

4 lb (2 kg) ripe tomatoes, coarsely chopped

6 oz (185 g) red (Spanish) onion, cut into pieces

1 tablespoon vegetable oil, plus oil for frying

1 tablespoon plus 1 teaspoon salt

1½ lb (750 g) swordfish, tuna, halibut or cod fillets, cut into 2- to 3-inch (5- to 7.5-cm) chunks

8 fresh epazote or cilantro (fresh coriander) sprigs, plus extra sprigs for garnish

24 corn tortillas

2 cups (16 fl oz/500 ml) puréed pot beans made from black beans (*recipe on page 11*)

8 fresh habanero or jalapeño chili peppers, roasted, peeled and cut into strips (*see glossary*)

Working in batches, place the tomatoes and onion in a blender or in a food processor fitted with the metal blade. Purée until smooth.

In a saucepan over high heat, warm the 1 tablespoon oil. Add the purée and the 1 tablespoon salt and cook uncovered, stirring often, until thickened, about 10 minutes. Cover and keep hot.

Meanwhile, in another saucepan combine the fish, the 8 epazote or cilantro sprigs and the 1 teaspoon salt. Add water to cover, place over low heat, and simmer until the fish flakes with a fork, about 20 minutes. Drain well and let cool. Using your fingers, shred the fish into a bowl, or mash with a fork. Add 3 cups (24 fl oz/750 ml) of the hot tomato sauce and mix well.

In a frying pan over high heat, pour in oil to a depth of ½ inch (12 mm). When the oil is hot, add the tortillas, one at a time, and fry, turning once, until soft, about 5 seconds on each side. Using tongs, transfer to paper towels to drain briefly.

To assemble the pies, gently heat the puréed beans in a heavy saucepan, adding water if necessary to form a thick sauce. Place a little of the tomato sauce on 8 individual plates. Working with 8 of the tortillas, dip them, one at a time, into the hot tomato sauce and then place on the plates. Cover each with about 2 tablespoons beans and then 2 heaping tablespoons of the fish mixture. Dip 8 more tortillas in the tomato sauce and place atop each serving. Repeat the bean and fish layers. Dip the final 8 tortillas in the sauce and place atop each serving. Spoon any remaining tomato sauce evenly over the top. Garnish with the roasted pepper strips and epazote or cilantro sprigs and serve.

Serves 8

Chili con Carne

4 dried ancho chili peppers

4 dried guajillo chili peppers or
    4 additional ancho chili peppers

4 cups (32 fl oz/1 l) water

2 tablespoons corn oil or other vegetable
    oil

1½ lb (750 g) lean ground (minced) beef

1 large onion, finely chopped

1 clove garlic, finely chopped

1 teaspoon paprika

1 teaspoon dried oregano, crumbled

1½ teaspoons ground cumin

1 tablespoon chili powder, or to taste

2 canned pickled jalapeño chili peppers,
    finely chopped

1 can (1 lb/500 g) plum (Roma) tomatoes,
    drained and coarsely chopped

1 can (1 lb/500 g) kidney beans, drained

salt

chopped onion, shredded Cheddar cheese
    and *totopos (recipe on page 9),* optional

This famous Tex-Mex dish was undoubtedly inspired by the meat-and-chili stews of Mexico. Beans are included in this version, making it a hearty one-dish meal. If you like, serve with white rice, a side salad, totopos *and cold beer.*

Rinse all the dried chilies and place in a saucepan with the water. Bring to a boil over high heat, reduce the heat to medium-low, cover and simmer until the chilies are soft, about 15 minutes. Drain, reserving the water, and, when cool enough to handle, stem the chilies.

In a food processor fitted with the metal blade or in a blender, place the softened chilies and 1½ cups (12 fl oz/375 ml) of their cooking water. Process to form a smooth purée. Set aside.

In a large saucepan over medium-high heat, warm the oil. Crumble in the beef and cook, stirring, until well browned, 5–7 minutes. Using a slotted spoon, transfer the meat to a bowl and set aside.

Reduce the heat to medium and add the onion and garlic to the pan. Sauté until the onion is translucent, 2–3 minutes. Return the meat to the pan and add the paprika, oregano, cumin, chili powder, jalapeños, tomatoes and the reserved chili purée. Bring to a boil, reduce the heat to medium-low and add the kidney beans. Cover and simmer, stirring often, until the mixture thickens, about 25 minutes. Season to taste with salt.

Serve hot. Accompany with bowls of chopped onion, shredded cheese and *totopos,* if desired, for diners to add to taste.

Serves 6

Tequila-Marinated Beef Fajitas
FAJITAS DE CARNE AL TEQUILA

3 lb (1.5 kg) skirt steak
½ cup (4 fl oz/125 ml) fresh lime juice
⅓ cup (3 fl oz/80 ml) plus 1 tablespoon
   corn oil or other vegetable oil
½ cup (4 fl oz/125 ml) tequila
1 teaspoon ground cumin
1 teaspoon dried oregano, crumbled
½ teaspoon freshly ground pepper
3 large cloves garlic, finely chopped
6 small onions, cut in half
18 flour or corn tortillas
3 cups (24 fl oz/750 ml) refried beans
   (recipe on page 11)
guacamole (recipe on page 25)
fresh Mexican salsa (recipe on page 12)
1 cup (8 fl oz/250 ml) sour cream
1 cup (1½ oz/45 g) finely chopped fresh
   cilantro (fresh coriander)

A tequila-herb marinade adds flavor to these popular steak-filled Tex-Mex soft tacos. Chicken may be used instead of beef, and the fajitas are also good cooked over a charcoal fire.

*T*rim the excess fat from the meat and cut the meat crosswise into long strips about ½ inch (12 mm) wide. Place the strips in a shallow nonreactive dish. In a bowl stir together the lime juice, the ⅓ cup (3 fl oz/80 ml) oil, tequila, cumin, oregano, pepper and garlic. Pour over the meat, coating each piece well. Cover with plastic wrap and refrigerate for 24 hours, turning the meat over a few times.

In a heavy frying pan or a griddle over medium heat, warm the 1 tablespoon oil. Add the onion halves and cook, stirring, until well browned, 6–8 minutes. Transfer to a plate and keep warm.

Place the same pan or griddle over high heat. Drain the meat well, reserving the marinade. Add the meat to the pan or griddle and cook, turning once and basting with the leftover marinade, until done to your liking, about 2 minutes on each side for medium-rare. Transfer to the plate holding the onions and keep warm.

Heat the tortillas, turning once, on the same pan or griddle, about 10 seconds on each side. Alternatively, wrap in plastic wrap and place in a microwave oven for about 30 seconds.

Just before serving, gently heat the refried beans in a heavy saucepan. Alternatively, place in a microwave-safe dish and heat in the microwave oven. Cover and keep warm.

Arrange the meat, onions and tortillas on a warmed platter. Place the refried beans, guacamole, salsa, sour cream and cilantro in separate dishes on the side. Each diner places some meat on a tortilla, adds the other ingredients as desired and then folds the tortilla in half and eats out of hand.

Serves 6–8

Chicken Enchiladas with Tomato-Chipotle Sauce

ENCHILADAS DE TOMATE CON CHIPOTLE

1 whole chicken breast or 2 breast halves

6 tomatoes

1 clove garlic

1 onion, cut up

1 canned chipotle chili pepper in red adobo sauce

1 tablespoon corn oil or other vegetable oil, plus oil for frying

18 corn tortillas

1 cup (4 oz/125 g) shredded Cheddar cheese

Instead of chicken, fill these classic baked enchiladas with leftover turkey or pork for an easy evening main course. Serve the enchiladas with guacamole (recipe on page 25) and refried beans (page 11).

Place the chicken in a saucepan with water to cover. Bring to a boil, reduce the heat to low, cover and simmer until tender, about 25 minutes. Drain well and let cool. Bone and skin the chicken, then, using your fingers or 2 forks, shred the meat. Set aside.

Heat a dry, heavy frying pan or griddle over medium heat. Roast the tomatoes and garlic on the pan or griddle, turning often, until well charred, about 3 minutes for the garlic and 4 minutes for the tomatoes. Coarsely chop the tomatoes.

In a blender or in a food processor fitted with the metal blade, combine the tomatoes, garlic, onion and chili. Purée until smooth. In a frying pan over high heat, warm the 1 tablespoon oil. Add the purée and cook, stirring, until thickened, about 5 minutes. Set aside.

Preheat an oven to 450°F (230°C). Butter a baking dish.

In a small frying pan over high heat, pour in oil to a depth of ½ inch (12 mm). When hot, fry the tortillas, one at a time, until soft, about 5 seconds on each side. Using tongs, transfer to paper towels to drain.

Dip each tortilla into the tomato sauce. Top with some of the chicken and then roll it into a cylinder. Place seam-side down in the baking dish. When all of the enchiladas have been formed, pour the remaining sauce over the top and sprinkle with the cheese. Bake until the cheese melts, about 10 minutes. Serve immediately.

Serves 6

Cuauhtémoc's Tortilla Pie

PASTEL CUAUHTÉMOC

2 whole chicken breasts or 4 breast halves

24 corn tortillas

corn oil or other vegetable oil for frying

2 cups (16 fl oz/500 ml) refried black beans (recipe on page 11)

¼ teaspoon ground cumin

2 cups (16 fl oz/500 ml) water

1 teaspoon salt

1 dried ancho chili pepper, soaked in warm water for 30 minutes and drained

3 poblano chili peppers, roasted, peeled and cut into long, thin strips (see glossary)

3 cups (12 oz/375 g) shredded Cheddar cheese

1 cup (8 fl oz/250 ml) thick sour cream (see glossary)

Fancifully named for the Aztec emperor in Spanish colonial days, this tortilla casserole combines very basic ingredients dating back to those early times. If you have day-old tortillas on hand, this recipe is a good way to use them. Serve it as a dinner main course or as a light lunch.

*P*lace the chicken in a saucepan with water to cover. Bring to a boil, reduce the heat to low, cover and simmer until tender, about 25 minutes. Drain well and let cool. Bone and skin the chicken, then, using your fingers or 2 forks, shred the meat. Set aside.

Preheat an oven to 400°F (200°C).

Cut off the dry edges from the tortillas, leaving the tortillas round. In a frying pan over high heat, pour in oil to a depth of ½ inch (12 mm). When the oil is hot, add the tortillas, one at a time, and fry, turning once, until soft, about 5 seconds on each side. Using tongs, transfer to paper towels to drain.

In a blender or in a food processor fitted with the metal blade, combine the refried beans, cumin, water, salt and the soaked ancho chili. Process to form a smooth purée.

Spoon enough of the purée into a 9-by-12-by-3-inch (23-by-30-by-7.5-cm) baking dish to cover the bottom. Layer half of the tortillas in the dish. Spoon half of the remaining purée over the top, then layer half each of the chicken, poblano chili strips and cheese. Repeat the layers, ending with cheese. Bake until the cheese melts and the pie is bubbling, about 25 minutes.

Let stand for 15–20 minutes, to allow the pie to settle before serving. Cover with the cream, cut into squares and serve.

Serves 6–8

Cheese-Stuffed Shrimp with Chipotle Sauce

CAMARONES RELLENOS CON SALSA CHIPOTLE

36 large fresh shrimp (prawns)

2 cups (8 oz/250 g) shredded mild
   Cheddar cheese

36 slices lean bacon

2 cups (16 fl oz/500 ml) thick sour cream
   (*see glossary*)

2 teaspoons liquid from canned chipotle
   chili peppers in red adobo sauce, or
   more to taste

corn oil or other vegetable oil for frying

2 lemons, thinly sliced

few fresh parsley sprigs

From Manzanillo in the state of Colima, this shrimp dish makes an elegant main course served with a mixture of white rice and peas. You can also enjoy the shrimp on their own as an hors d'oeuvre or first course.

✧

*P*eel each shrimp, then devein by making a lengthwise slit along the outside curve and removing the dark intestinal vein. Butterfly the shrimp by deepening the slit, but do not cut all the way through.

Place about 1 tablespoon of the cheese between the shrimp halves, pressing it firmly so it fills the cavity fully. Starting from the head end and working toward the tail, wrap the bacon around the shrimp, making sure the cheese is completely covered. Tack the end of the bacon to the shrimp with a toothpick. Place the shrimp on a tray and place in the freezer for about 1 hour, to chill well. (This prevents the cheese from melting too quickly during cooking.)

Combine the cream and chipotle chili liquid in a small bowl and stir to mix well. Set aside.

In a deep-fat fryer or large, deep heavy frying pan, pour in oil to a depth of 2 inches (5 cm) and heat to 375°F (190°C), or until a small piece of onion sizzles immediately upon being dropped in the oil. When the oil is ready, add the shrimp, a few at a time to prevent sticking, and fry until the bacon is crisp and browned, 2–3 minutes. Using a slotted spoon, transfer to paper towels to drain.

Serve hot on individual dishes topped with the chipotle-cream sauce, or on a platter with the sauce in a dish on the side. Garnish with the lemon slices and parsley sprigs.

Serves 6

Chicken Enchiladas with Peanut-Almond Sauce

ENCHILADAS DE POLLO CON SALSA DE NUECES

1 large whole chicken breast or 2 breast halves

⅔ cup (3½ oz/100 g) plus ¼ cup (1½ oz/ 45 g) peanut halves

⅔ cup (3½ oz/100 g) blanched whole almonds

6 dried ancho chili peppers, seeded, deribbed and cut into pieces

3 tablespoons sesame seeds

½ onion, cut up

2 cloves garlic

1 slice white or whole-wheat (wholemeal) bread, soaked briefly in distilled white vinegar, drained and lightly squeezed

2 tablespoons corn oil or other vegetable oil, plus oil for frying

18 corn tortillas

A sauce of peanuts, almonds and ancho chilies, typical of Guanajuato in central Mexico, richly coats these chicken enchiladas. Turkey or pork may be substituted. Serve them with rice or refried beans (recipe on page 11).

*P*lace the chicken in a saucepan with water to cover. Bring to a boil, reduce the heat to low, cover and simmer until tender, about 25 minutes. Drain well and let cool. Bone and skin the chicken, then, using your fingers or 2 forks, shred the meat. Set aside.

In a frying pan over medium heat, toast ⅔ cup (3½ oz/100 g) each peanuts and almonds, shaking the pan occasionally, until golden, about 5 minutes. Transfer to a blender or to a food processor fitted with the metal blade. In the same pan, toast the chilies and sesame seeds, shaking the pan occasionally, until the seeds are golden, about 3 minutes. Add to the nuts, along with the onion, garlic and bread. Purée until thick.

In a frying pan over medium heat, warm the 2 tablespoons oil. Add the purée and boil gently uncovered, stirring, to blend the flavors, about 5 minutes. Add water if the mixture is too thick for dipping tortillas. Cover and keep warm over low heat.

In a frying pan over high heat, pour in oil to a depth of ½ inch (12 mm). When hot, fry the tortillas, one at a time and turning once, just until softened, about 5 seconds on each side. Using tongs, transfer to paper towels to drain briefly. Dip the tortillas, one at a time, into the sauce and fill each tortilla with some of the chicken. Fold in half and arrange on a warmed serving platter or individual plates. Cover with the remaining sauce and garnish with the ¼ cup (1½ oz/45 g) peanut halves. Serve immediately.

Serves 6

Swiss Enchiladas

ENCHILADAS SUIZAS

2 whole chicken breasts or 4 breast halves

1 large onion

6 peppercorns

3 bay leaves

salt to taste, plus 1 teaspoon salt

freshly ground pepper

2 lb (1 kg) tomatillos, husks removed

2 cloves garlic

3 tablespoons coarsely chopped fresh
cilantro (fresh coriander)

2 or 3 fresh jalapeño or serrano chili
peppers, seeded

¼ cup (2 fl oz/60 ml) corn oil or other
vegetable oil, plus oil for frying

12 corn tortillas

3 cups (12 oz/375 g) shredded Cheddar
cheese

1 cup (8 fl oz/250 ml) thick sour cream
(see glossary)

*Long ago, some unsung Swiss cook gave his or her nationality to the name
for this Mexican dish of baked enchiladas topped with cheese and cream.*

*I*n a large saucepan over high heat, combine the chicken, ⅓ of the
onion, the peppercorns, bay leaves, salt to taste and water to cover.
Bring to a boil, reduce the heat to low, cover and simmer until the
chicken is tender, about 25 minutes. Remove the chicken from the
broth; strain the broth, reserving 2 cups (16 fl oz/500 ml). Let the
chicken cool, then bone and skin. Using your fingers or 2 forks,
shred the meat, then season to taste with salt and pepper. Set aside.

Place the tomatillos in a saucepan over high heat and add water to
cover. Bring to a boil, reduce the heat to low and simmer until soft,
about 10 minutes. Drain and let cool completely.

In a blender or in a food processor fitted with the metal blade,
combine the tomatillos, the remaining ⅔ onion (cut up), the garlic,
cilantro and chilies. Process to form a smooth purée.

In a large saucepan over high heat, warm the ¼ cup (2 fl oz/60 ml)
oil. Add the tomatillo purée and cook, stirring, until thickened, 2–3
minutes. Add the reserved broth and the 1 teaspoon salt, cover and
simmer over low heat until the sauce is reduced, about 15 minutes.

Meanwhile, preheat an oven to 400°F (200°C). In a frying pan
over high heat, pour in oil to a depth of ½ inch (12 mm). Fry the
tortillas, one at a time and turning once, until they begin to soften,
3–5 seconds on each side. Drain on paper towels.

Grease a large baking dish or 4 or 6 individual gratin dishes. Place
some of the chicken on each tortilla, roll up into a cylinder and
place seam-side down in the prepared dish(es). Cover with the
tomatillo sauce and top with the cheese. Bake until the cheese melts,
15–20 minutes. Pour on the cream just before serving.

Serves 4–6

Pork Enchiladas with Poblano Chili Sauce

ENCHILADAS POBLANAS

FOR THE PORK:

10 oz (315 g) pork tenderloin, in one
    piece
1 clove garlic
¼ small onion
½ teaspoon salt
3 cups (24 fl oz/750 ml) water

FOR THE POBLANO CHILI SAUCE:

3 fresh poblano chili peppers, about 6 oz
    (180 g) total weight, roasted, peeled and
    chopped (see glossary)
½ cup (4 fl oz/125 ml) milk
1 clove garlic
1 teaspoon salt
3 cups (24 fl oz/750 ml) thick sour cream
    (see glossary)
2 tablespoons corn oil or other vegetable
    oil, plus oil for frying
1 tablespoon minced onion

12 corn tortillas
⅔ cup (3½ oz/100 g) crumbled *queso
    fresco* or feta cheese
4 romaine lettuce leaves, shredded
    (optional)
1 ripe avocado, halved, pitted, peeled
    and sliced
3 or 4 radishes, sliced

The deep green, tapered poblano chili imparts its distinctive flavor to this attractive supper dish. Serve with refried beans (recipe on page 11), Mexican rice, a simple salad and beer.

*T*o prepare the pork, in a saucepan over high heat, combine the pork, garlic, onion, salt and water. Bring to a boil, reduce the heat, cover and simmer until the pork is tender, about 40 minutes. Remove the pork from the broth and let cool. Using your fingers, shred the meat and set aside.

To make the chili sauce, in a blender or in a food processor fitted with the metal blade, combine the chilies, milk, garlic and salt. Process to form a smooth purée, then transfer to a bowl. Add the cream and stir to mix well.

In a frying pan over medium heat, warm the 2 tablespoons oil. Add the onion and fry until lightly golden, about 2 minutes. Add the chili sauce and simmer, uncovered, until the mixture thickens slightly, about 10 minutes. Cover and keep warm over very low heat.

In a frying pan over high heat, pour in oil to a depth of ½ inch (12 mm). When the oil is hot, add the tortillas, one at a time, and fry, turning once, until they begin to soften, about 5 seconds on each side. Using tongs, transfer to paper towels to drain briefly.

Dip the fried tortillas, one at a time, into the poblano-cream sauce and top each tortilla with an equal amount of the shredded pork. Fold in half and arrange on a warmed serving platter.

Cover the tortillas with the remaining sauce and garnish with the cheese, lettuce (if desired), avocado and radishes. Serve immediately.

Serves 6

Glossary

The following glossary defines terms specifically as they relate to Mexican cooking, including major and unusual ingredients and basic techniques.

AVOCADO

The finest-flavored variety of this popular vegetable-fruit is the Haas, which has a pearlike shape and a thick, bumpy, dark green skin. Ripe, ready-to-use avocados will yield slightly to fingertip pressure.

To remove the pit neatly, first, using a sharp knife, cut down to the pit lengthwise all around the avocado. Gently twist the halves in opposite directions to separate; lift away the half without the pit.

Cup the half with the pit in the palm of one hand, with your fingers and thumb safely clear. Hold a sturdy, sharp knife with the other hand and strike the pit with the blade of the knife, wedging the blade firmly into the pit. Then twist and lift the knife to remove the pit.

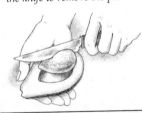

BEANS

Beans are a popular form of carbohydrates and protein in Mexican cooking. Before use, dried beans should be carefully picked over to remove any impurities such as small stones or fibers or any discolored or misshapen beans. Next, to rehydrate them and thus shorten their cooking time and improve their digestibility, whole beans are often soaked in cold water to cover generously for a few hours.

Scores of different kinds of beans are used in cuisines worldwide; the most common varieties for Mexican cooking include:

Black Beans
Earthy-tasting, mealy-textured beans, relatively small in size and with deep black skins. Also called turtle beans.

Kidney Beans
Widely popular, kidney-shaped beans with brownish-red skins, slightly mealy texture and robust flavor. Also sold precooked in cans. White kidney beans are also available.

Pink Beans
Meaty-flavored, mealy-textured beans with pinkish brown skins. Pinto or kidney beans may be substituted.

Pinto Beans
Full-flavored, mealy-textured beans with distinctively mottled brown-and-tan skins. Similarly patterned cranberry beans may be substituted.

BELL PEPPER
Fresh, sweet-fleshed, bell-shaped member of the pepper family. Also known as capsicum. Most common in the unripe green form, although ripened red or yellow varieties are also available. Creamy pale yellow, orange and purple-black types may also be found.

CHEESES
Cheese is a popular ingredient and garnish in Mexican cuisine. The most popular varieties include:

American
Processed, mild, Cheddar-style cheese; appreciated for its good melting properties.

Cheddar Cheese
Firm, smooth whole-milk cheese, pale yellow-white to deep yellow-orange and ranging in taste from mild and sweet when fresh to rich and sharply tangy when aged.

Feta
Crumbly Greek-style cheese made from goat's or sheep's milk, notable for its salty, slightly sharp flavor. An acceptable substitute for Mexican *queso fresco*.

Monterey Jack
Mild, slightly tangy semisoft cheese made from whole, partly skimmed or skimmed cow's milk.

Parmesan
Hard, thick-crusted Italian cow's milk cheese with a sharp, salty, full flavor resulting from at least two years of aging. Buy in block form, to grate fresh as needed, rather than already grated. The finest Italian variety is designated parmigiano-reggiano.

Pecorino
Italian sheep's milk cheese, sold either fresh or aged. Two of its most popular aged forms are pecorino romano and pecorino sardo; the latter cheese is tangier than the former.

Queso Fresco
Literally, "fresh cheese." Soft, crumbly fresh cow's milk cheese used to garnish many Mexican dishes. Also known as *queso blanco*. Available in Hispanic markets in large cities. Mild feta cheese may be substituted.

CHILI POWDER
Commercial blend of spices featuring ground dried **chili peppers** along with such other seasonings as **cumin, oregano,** cloves, **coriander,** pepper and salt. Best purchased in small quantities, because flavor diminishes rapidly after opening.

CHILI SAUCE
Commercial bottled blend of hot and mild **chili peppers,** vinegar, sugar and other flavorings, used as a seasoning ingredient or as a condiment.

CHORIZO
Mexican- or Spanish-style coarse-textured pork sausage spiced with hot **chilies** and other seasonings. Available in Latin American food stores and meat markets and in better food markets.

CILANTRO
Green, leafy herb resembling flat-leaf (Italian) parsley, with a sharp, aromatic, somewhat astringent flavor. Also called fresh coriander or Chinese parsley.

CHILI PEPPERS

A wide variety of chilies in fresh, dried, bottled and canned forms may be found in well-stocked food stores and ethnic markets.

Fresh Chilies

Common fresh chilies used in this book include:

Habanero

Incendiary green or ripened chili, estimated to be at least 30 times hotter than the jalapeño.

Jalapeño

Small, thick-fleshed, fiery chili (above, right), usually sold green, although red ripened specimens may sometimes be found. Also available pickled in brine or smoke-dried to make chipotle chilies, which are sold dried, canned in vinegar or, most commonly, in a thick vinegar-based adobo sauce.

Pasilla

Dark green to black chili when fresh and dark brown when dried. Moderately hot and with a hint of berry flavor. In fresh form sometimes labeled chilaca.

Poblano

Mild-to-hot dark green chili that resembles a tapered, triangular bell pepper.

Serrano

Small, slender, very hot green chili (below) also sold in its ripened red form and pickled in brine.

Yellow Chilies

Specimens such as the Hungarian wax chili, the banana chili or the Santa Fe grande measure 3–5 inches (7.5–13 cm) in length and have slightly sweet, moderate-to-hot flesh.

Dried Chilies

Once red and ripened, chilies are commonly preserved by drying. Dried chilies are often soaked in water to cover, thus softening them for easier blending. Varieties used in this book include:

Ancho

Dried ripened poblano chili (below), fruity and moderately hot.

Guajillo

Long, tapered, deep orange-red chili with a sharp, slightly sweet, mildly hot taste.

Handling chilies

When handling any chili, fresh or dried, wear kitchen gloves to prevent any cuts or abrasions on your hands from contacting the pepper's volatile oils; wash your hands well with warm, soapy water, and take special care not to touch your eyes or any other sensitive areas.

Seeding a fresh chili

The seeds and white ribs found inside a chili are intensely hot, and are often removed before the chili is used. If a recipe calls for stuffing a chili, simply cut a slit along its length with a small, sharp knife; then carefully use the knife tip to scrape out the seeds and ribs. If the chili will be cut up, use the following procedure:

1. Cut the chili in half lengthwise. With your fingers, or using the knife blade, remove and discard the tough stem.

2. Use the tip of the knife to scrape out the seeds and cut out the ribs, cutting into the flesh of the chili to remove all the pale parts.

Roasting chilies

Chilies may be roasted to develop their flavor while also softening their flesh and loosening their skins. They may be roasted by several different methods, including turning them in a frying pan over moderate heat, frying them in oil, baking them in a hot oven, or broiling or grilling them. One of the easiest methods, however, is to roast them directly over a gas flame:

1. Set the flame to medium. Grasp a chili with a long-handled fork or a pair of metal kitchen tongs. Turn the chili over the flame (above, right) until its skin is completely blistered, 5–10 minutes depending upon the pepper's size.

2. Cover the chili with a kitchen towel or place in a paper bag and let it sweat until cool enough to handle, 10–15 minutes.

3. Then, using your fingertips, peel off all the blistered skin. Carefully cut open the chili and remove the stem, seeds and ribs. If the chili is a very spicy variety, you can reduce its fieriness by then soaking for at least 40 minutes in a mixture of 1 cup (8 fl oz/250 ml) water, 1 tablespoon distilled white vinegar and 2 teaspoons salt.

CONSOMMÉ, CANNED BEEF
Concentrated form of clear beef stock or broth, used as a cooking liquid and source of rich flavor.

CORIANDER SEEDS
Small, ridged, pale yellow to yellow-brown seeds of the herb **cilantro,** used whole or ground to add a subtly sharp, slightly sweet edge of flavor.

CORN HUSKS, DRIED
The leaves that enwrap an ear of corn, dried to form flat, thin, pale brown husks. Most commonly used as wrappers for tamales. Sold in plastic packages in well-stocked food stores and ethnic markets.

CORN KERNELS
Before use, fresh sweet corn must be stripped of its green outer husks and the fine inner silky threads must be removed. If a recipe calls for removing the raw kernels from an ear of corn, hold the ear by its pointed end, steadying its stalk end on a cutting board.

Use a sharp, sturdy knife to cut down and away from you along the ear, stripping off the kernels from the cob. Continue turning the ear with each cut.

CRAB MEAT
Already-cooked crab meat is widely available in fish markets or the seafood counters of quality food markets. Most often, it has been frozen; for best flavor and texture, seek out fresh crab meat.

CREAM
Sour Cream
Commercial dairy product, made from pasteurized sweet cream, with a tangy flavor and thick consistency. Used as a rich garnish for a variety of savory Mexican recipes.
Thick Sour Cream
When "thick sour cream" is called for in recipes, it refers to a thick, slightly sour cream similar to French crème fraîche. To make your own, stir 2 tablespoons sour cream, buttermilk or plain yogurt into 1 cup (8 fl oz/250 ml) heavy (double) cream, cover with plastic wrap and let stand in a warm place until thickened, 8–24 hours. Stir and refrigerate. It will keep for up to 1 week. It will have better flavor if it is allowed to age in the refrigerator for several days. If you do not have time to prepare thick sour cream, use regular sour cream.

CUMIN
Spice native to the Middle East, with a strong, dusky, aromatic flavor.

EPAZOTE
Pungent annual herb, possibly indigenous to Mexico, which has no substitute for its unusual flavor. Although seldom available commercially outside Mexico, except in India, it is easily grown from seed and is self-sowing. Both seeds and plants are available from some specialty plant catalogs. It can be used dried, after the twigs are discarded, but the flavor is greatly diminished.

JICAMA
Large Mexican tuber with light brown skin concealing crisp, juicy, slightly sweet ivory flesh comparable to water chestnuts. Usually eaten raw.

LARD
Although the rendered fat of the pig is the traditional cooking fat of Mexico, it is essential in only a few dishes; vegetable oil may be substituted. Use real lard rather than the processed hydrogenated kind sold in most food markets. It is easy to render your own: Chop small pieces of pork fat in a food processor and put in a roasting pan in a 250°F (130°C) oven until melted. Strain and store in the refrigerator for up to 1 month.

LIME
The common lime in Mexico resembles the small, smooth-skinned Key lime rather than the larger, sweeter, dark green Persian lime found in other parts of the world. Lime wedges garnish many recipes in Mexico, much like lemons—seldom found in Mexico—do elsewhere.

MAGGI SAUCE
Commercial brand of liquid vegetable extract, similar in flavor to concentrated beef bouillon, used to enhance the taste of sauces and other savory preparations. Widely available in food stores.

MANGO
Tropical fruit with a juicy, aromatic orange flesh. Ripe mangoes yield slightly to finger pressure; ripen firm mangoes at room temperature in an open paper or plastic bag. The skin peels easily when slit with a knife. Slice the flesh from both sides of the large, flat pit, as well as from around its edges.

MASA HARINA
Commercial flour ground from treated field corn, for use in making **tortillas,** tamales and other corn-based specialties. The most common and reliable brand is Quaker. Regular cornmeal is not an acceptable substitute.

OIL
For frying in most Mexican recipes, use a flavorless oil capable of being heated to high temperatures, such as vegetable or corn oil. Olive oil, on the other hand, may be used when its distinctive flavor is preferred; extra-virgin olive oil, extracted from olives on the first pressing without use of heat or chemicals, is most highly prized for its pure, fruity taste and golden to pale green hue.

OLIVES, GREEN
Olives picked in their unripened green state and cured in brine—sometimes with seasonings, vinegars and oils—to produce results generally more sharp tasting than ripe black olives. Sold in ethnic delicatessens, specialty-food shops and well-stocked supermarkets.

ONIONS
Several kinds of onions add flavor to traditional Mexican dishes. Green onions, also called spring onions or scallions, are a variety harvested immature, leaves and all, before their bulbs have formed. The green and white parts may both be enjoyed, raw or cooked, for their mild but still pronounced onion flavor. Red (Spanish) onions are a mild, sweet

variety with purplish red skin and red-tinged white flesh. Yellow onions are the common, white-fleshed, strong-flavored variety distinguished by their dry, yellowish brown skins. White-fleshed onions with white skins have a sharper flavor than yellow onions and are preferred by Mexican cooks.

OREGANO
Aromatic, pungent and spicy Mediterranean herb—also known as wild marjoram—used fresh or dried as a seasoning for all kinds of savory dishes. Especially complements tomatoes and other vegetables.

PUMPKIN SEEDS
Oval, flat, green seeds of the common pumpkin, known in Mexico as *pepitas*. Toasted and removed from their white husks, they are eaten as a snack in Mexico, or they are ground and added to sauces and other dishes to contribute rich flavor and body. Available in health-food stores and well-stocked food stores.

RADISHES
Crisp root vegetable, usually eaten raw and prized for its refreshing flavor characterized by a pungent, peppery hotness that varies from mild to assertive, depending upon the variety.

SHORTENING, VEGETABLE
Solid vegetable fat sometimes used in place of or in combination with butter or **lard** in batters or doughs. The fat is said to "shorten" the flour, that is, to make it flaky and tender. May also be used for deep-frying.

SOY SAUCE
Asian seasoning and condiment made from soybeans, wheat, salt and water. Seek out good-quality imported soy sauces; Chinese brands tend to be markedly saltier than Japanese.

TEQUILA
The best-known Mexican spirit, a powerful, clear or golden liquid distilled from the juice of the blue agave (century) plant.

TOMATILLOS
The small, green tomatillo (below) resembles—but is not actually

related to—the tomato. Fresh tomatillos, available in some Latin American markets and well-stocked food markets, usually come encased in brown papery husks, easily peeled off before tomatillos are cut. Canned tomatillos may be found in specialty-food sections of markets.

TOMATOES
During the summer, when tomatoes are in season, use the best sun-ripened tomatoes you can find. At other times of the year, plum tomatoes, sometimes called Roma or egg tomatoes, are likely to have the best flavor and texture.

To peel fresh tomatoes, first bring a saucepan of water to a boil. Using a small, sharp knife, cut out the core from the stem end of the tomato. Then cut a shallow X in the skin at the tomato's base. Submerge for about 20 seconds in the boiling water, then remove and dip in a bowl of cold water. Starting at the X, peel the skin from the tomato, using your fingertips and, if necessary, the knife blade. Cut the tomatoes in half and turn each half cut-side down. Then cut as directed in individual recipes.

To seed a tomato, cut it in half crosswise. Squeeze gently to force out the seed sacks.

TORTILLAS
Thin, flat, round unleavened Mexican bread made from wheat flour or finely ground cornmeal; used as an edible wrapper for meat, poultry, seafood, cheese and other foods. Commercially manufactured tortillas are widely available in food stores and ethnic markets.

VINEGAR
Literally "sour" wine, vinegar results when certain strains of yeast cause wine—or some other alcoholic liquid such as apple cider—to ferment for a second time, turning it acidic. Distilled white vinegar is fermented from grain-mash alcohol, resulting in a clear, colorless liquid that adds acidity without contributing a distinctive flavor of its own.

WORCESTERSHIRE SAUCE
Traditional English seasoning or condiment; an intensely flavorful, savory and aromatic blend of many ingredients, including molasses, **soy sauce**, garlic, onion and anchovies. Popular as a marinade ingredient or table sauce for grilled foods, especially red meats.

SHRIMP
Peeling and Deveining
Fresh, raw shrimp (prawns) are usually sold with the heads already removed but the shells still intact. Before cooking, they are often peeled and their thin, veinlike intestinal tracts removed. After deveining, large shrimp are frequently butterflied to help them cook more evenly.

1. With your thumbs, split open the shrimp's shell along the concave side, between its two rows of legs. Peel away the shell, taking care to leave the last segment with tail fin intact and attached to the meat.

2. Using a small, sharp knife, carefully make a shallow slit along the peeled shrimp's back, just deep enough to expose the long, usually dark-colored, veinlike intestinal tract. With the tip of the knife or your fingers, lift up and pull out the vein, discarding it.

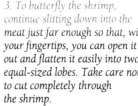

3. To butterfly the shrimp, continue slitting down into the meat just far enough so that, with your fingertips, you can open it out and flatten it easily into two equal-sized lobes. Take care not to cut completely through the shrimp.

Index

ACKNOWLEDGMENTS

The publishers would like to thank the following people and organizations for their generous assistance and support in producing this book:
Adelfa Silva, Ma. de la Luz Espinoza, Rosario Madero, Laura Rebolledo, Anne Hoffmann-Pinther, Baronessa Sandra di Portanova, Rosa Maria Iglesias, Sharon C. Lott, Stephen W. Griswold, Tara Brown, Ken DellaPenta, the buyers for Gardener's Eden, and the buyers and store managers for Pottery Barn and Williams-Sonoma stores.

The following kindly lent props for the photography:
Biordi Art Imports, J. Goldsmith Antiques, Fillamento, Fredericksen Hardware, Forrest Jones, Stephanie Greenleigh, Sue Fisher King, Lorraine & Judson Puckett, Waterford/Wedgwood, Sue White and Chuck Williams.